47 Mind Hacks for Writers

Master the Writing Habit in 10 Minutes Or Less and End Writer's Block and Procrastination for Good

By

Karen Dimmick & Steve Dimmick

Michael Grace Publishing LLC
1366 Grantham Dr, Sarasota, FL 34234.
Bookthority.com

First edition.
Printed in the United States of America.
ISBN: 978-1540771391

Published by Michael Grace Publishing LLC.
Edited by Ine de Baerdemaeker.
Book Cover Design by Shankha Ghosh.
Interior Book Design by Michael Grace Publishing LLC.
Interior Book Formatting by Gerard Galvis.

Disclaimer
While the publisher and author have made every attempt to verify that the information provided in this book is correct and up to date at the time of publication, the publisher and author assume no responsibility for any error, inaccuracy, or omission. Further, neither the publisher nor author have any control over and do not assume any responsibility for the websites or their content of the third-party websites mentioned in this book. The materials contained herein are not intended to represent or guarantee you will achieve your desired results, and the publisher and author make no such guarantee. Neither the publisher nor author shall be liable for damages arising therefrom.

What If Your Writing Was Unleashed?

No more procrastinating. No more interruptions. No more feeling like you're not good enough to be the writer you long to be. No more conflicts with family. No more writer's block. No more excuses.

The content of this book (and the companion material) will forever make you a more productive writer.

We asked over 100 authors and writers what their biggest obstacles were to being the writer they want to be.

This book will help you overcome your biggest challenges with 47 mind hacks:

- Put an end to writer's block… forever
- Uncover the real reason you're procrastinating and start writing today
- Discover a fun way to get your family to help you reach your writing goals
- Stop feeling like you're not good enough
- Shut down the overly-critical self-talk that holds you back

Plus, 43 other mind hacks, some of which will solve obstacles you don't even realize you have.

What Others Are Saying

"This book is an absolute treasure trove of ideas for winning the mental game of being a writer. Whether you want to finally finish your book, feel more confident about your writing, or think more like a marketer, this book can help you. In a word: Fantastic!"

Dana Wilde, Author & Host of the Mind Aware Show

"Essential reading for writers ready to go pro."

Tom Morkes, CEO Insurgent Publishing

"Of all the roadblocks that stand in a writer's way, none are more deadly than limiting beliefs. Thoughts of "I'm not good enough" or "I'll never" or "What if?" do more than stop creatives in their tracks. They rob the world of beautiful stories and life-changing ideas that never see the light of day. In this book, Karen and Steve offer meaningful steps to overcome limiting beliefs and get on with the job of creating. Wise, compassionate and practical, their advice can help writers shed their repetitive thoughts of disaster and inadequacy, and move on with freedom and joy. "

Jon Bard, Co-Owner Children's Book Insider

Your 11 Free Gifts

As a thank you for buying this book, we're offering 11 FREE resources:

1. Workbook
2. Private Facebook Group
3. Example 567 MP3 Recording
4. Fail Fast Process Guide
5. Pick Up Plan
6. Find the Gap Template
7. Street Teams: The Expert Interview
8. Gamification Buy In Template
9. List of Writing Apps
10. Adjusting Your Response MP3
11. Sales Tracking Template

Go to the link below to get instant access:
47MindHacks.com/FreeGift

Table of Contents

Getting the Most Out of This Book

This book is designed to provide a complete reader experience. While the book can stand alone, throughout this book there are links to additional content and resources. These provide a deeper learning experience and help you cement the belief changes you'll have so you can become a more effective writer.

Get The 47 Mind Hacks for Writers Workbook

There is an accompanying workbook for this book. It is designed to help you keep track of your progress and mindset changes for all the beliefs covered in this book. You can download it from 47MindHacks.com/Workbook.

Who Is This Book For?

This book is for authors and writers (or those who wish they were), who are letting limiting beliefs get in the way of their dreams.

If you struggle with your inner critic or handling other people's criticism, this book is for you. If you can't quite find the time to write, this book is for you. If you're afraid to put yourself out there, stand out from the crowd, and put your ideas out into the world – this book is for you.

In short, whether you are writing a work of fiction, a nonfiction book, a paper, or even a blog post, you will benefit from examining your current beliefs. If a limiting belief, lack of confidence, or an excuse (however valid) is holding you back from doing the writing you want to do, then this book is for you.

Introduction

"If you change your mind,
you can change your life."
William James (Philosopher, Psychologist)

Writing is like playing golf. You're not competing against someone else; you're competing against yourself and your subconscious mind. Just like golfers, writers experience ups and downs similar to riding a roller coaster. Those ups and downs never completely disappear, not even for the highly successful authors we all look up to.

The key to success, as a writer, is maximizing the 'up' times and minimizing the length, depth, and effect of the 'down' times. That's where being able to control your subconscious mind comes in. The fewer limiting beliefs you have, the fewer 'down' times you experience. While down times are inevitable, the more you can limit their effect, the faster you can get back to those 'up' times where you're in the zone and your writing, and life, are great.

When the idea for this book came to me, I started asking every writer and want-to-be writer I knew about the limiting beliefs that held them back. This book gives you a mind hack for every one of those self-imposed limits. Each chapter helps you overcome a negative belief or attitude that is stopping you from succeeding. All you have to do is read it. It's designed to speak directly to your subconscious and remove the limit. Are you struggling with beliefs like, "I'm not good enough," or, "This is all rubbish and I'm kidding myself," or "Why would anyone want to read what I write?" Then read on, and find out how to hack your inner critic's mind.

When it comes to promoting your book and approaching an influencer in your field, writers can suddenly lose all their confidence or come up against the limit of, "Why would they want to meet with me?" There are exercises and chapters in this book that help you throw those problems out of the window.

Anytime you want to feel confident, it's possible to literally flip the switch in as little as a couple of minutes. You don't need to believe something to do it; you can be as skeptical as you like. However, if you follow the exercise, even just because you want to prove it's wrong, you'll quickly see how powerful your subconscious mind is and just how much you can control that inner voice. And remember, you, and you alone, can control it. No other person has that control over you. As Eleanor Roosevelt so brilliantly said, "No one can make you feel inferior without your consent." The same goes for every single thought or emotion you feel. Everything is a choice. Your choice. The question is, are you going to make that choice and start controlling your subconscious mind? Or are you going to carry on and let it control your thoughts and emotions, put you through crushing self-doubt, and hold you back from what you want to achieve in your writing career? The choice is yours.

One of my favorite sayings from my journey as a writer is that "99% is a nightmare, 100% is a breeze". Sure, the original phrase was a little more colorful than that, but the essence is the same. It's about commitment. If you commit to something 99% of the way, that 1% will continually bite you. Every time something comes up, you have to ask yourself whether this time is the 1% and you should go do whatever it is instead of writing. It becomes a battle of willpower, which you, like all of us, will ultimately lose. Your life becomes a nightmare because of that mental tug of war.

However, when you commit 100%, life is infinitely easier. The answer to questions like, "Should I go to that party or should I write?" becomes obvious. You write. You're 100% committed, there's no option. That is the level of commitment you want to get to if you want to write. It's all or nothing. Anything else will result in no book. So if you're ready, make the decision to commit to writing a book and becoming an author. If you're not, then put that dream aside until you are.

If you've decided to start writing, you're currently writing, or you're already a published author, then I look forward to helping you get your mind in the right place to make your writing successful, faster, and more enjoyable. Welcome to *47 Mind Hacks for Writers*.

Success Mindset

*"Think boldly. Don't be afraid of
making mistakes. Be modest in
everything except your aims."*
Albert Szent-Györgyi (Nobel Prize Winner)

There are certain beliefs and attitudes successful authors have in their mindset that yet-to-be successful authors are missing.

In doing the research for this section, I came across an interesting belief from someone that, "No one reads anymore." Having read three books so far this week, I can assure you that people do still read. After all, you're reading this. However, let's look at Amazon for some hard facts.

All books are given an Amazon sales rank. While no one knows precisely how it works (since Amazon is good at keeping it secret), enough successful authors have tied together their book's rank and the number of copies they've sold to work out roughly what the ranks mean in terms of sales. Just looking at the top five books, of the several million they have listed, we can see:

1. #1 Book has roughly 6,400 sales a day
2. #2 Book has roughly 5,800 sales a day
3. #3 Book has roughly 5,200 sales a day
4. #4 Book has roughly 4,600 sales a day
5. #5 Book has roughly 4,000 sales a day

So just for the top five books, that's a total of 26,000 books sold each day. Sure, maybe not every single copy is getting read, but I think it's a fair assumption that 90% of them are. That means, just with those five books, 23,400 people are reading each day. And, like I said, Amazon has millions of books for sale. If people didn't read them, they would stop buying them. Since that hasn't happened, it's safe to say that, even with all the videos and podcasts out there, people do still read.

What about self-published books, though? Another interesting belief I came across was that, "Self-publishing would doom a book to obscurity."

If we look at the latest report from AuthorEarnings.com[1], Indie-published eBooks account for 43% (and rising) of all eBook sales on Amazon. The big five publishers account for only 23% (and falling). The rest are from small to medium publishers (17%), Amazon-published authors (10%), and publishers with a single author (7%). So, not only does self-publishing not mean a book will descend into obscurity, but Indie authors as a whole are selling nearly twice as many eBooks as the big five publishing houses on Amazon.

The report also gives statistics on what they call the '$100,000 club'. This is made up of authors who earn six figures or more from all formats of their book. There are a total of 1,340 authors who achieve this feat just from their Amazon sales. If we look at recent authors only, i.e. people who've become authors within the last five years, 425 of them are self-published indie authors. Only 115 of them are published by one of the big five publishers.

I'd say that is pretty conclusive evidence that self-publishing is not just a viable option, but actually an extremely wise choice for a new writer. Yes, there are still pros and cons to each method, but the belief that sub-publishing will doom your book is most definitely busted.

So let's jump into the mindset you'll need for success.

Mind Hack #1:

Taking the First Step

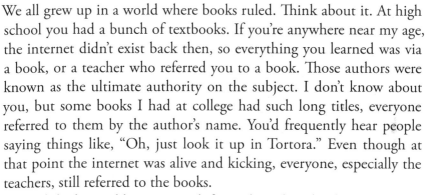

*"Living is a form of not being sure,
not knowing what next or how. We
guess. We may be wrong, but we
take leap after leap in the dark."*

Agnes de Mille (Choreographer)

We all grew up in a world where books ruled. Think about it. At high school you had a bunch of textbooks. If you're anywhere near my age, the internet didn't exist back then, so everything you learned was via a book, or a teacher who referred you to a book. Those authors were known as the ultimate authority on the subject. I don't know about you, but some books I had at college had such long titles, everyone referred to them by the author's name. You'd frequently hear people saying things like, "Oh, just look it up in Tortora." Even though at that point the internet was alive and kicking, everyone, especially the teachers, still referred to the books.

While the world moves much faster these days, books are still seen as that fount of knowledge. You know the benefits of having a book to your name: interviews on podcasts, radio shows, and maybe even on TV. You know the resulting authority will benefit your business and open up countless opportunities. And you know you might even get another stream of income from it. Even though you know all that, the days go by, one after the other, without you starting your book. The question is, "What's stopping you?"

One set of beliefs I hear variations on a lot is, "I'm too old (or too young)," "I haven't got my business going enough yet," and so on. Basically, you think it's too late (or too soon) to start. Well, I have news for you. I've met authors who are in their early teens (one pre-teen) and I've met authors in their late seventies, and just about every age between. If they can do it, it's possible. This means you can do it too, if you put your mind to it and decide to start.

What about the beliefs, "I'm not well known enough to write a book," or, "I don't have a business or a list yet, how can I possibly launch successfully?" Again, I've seen authors who start with nothing. That's the position we were in when we did our first book. We had zero followers. We were pretty much unknown in our field and hadn't yet started the business we planned to create around the book. I've equally seen authors with huge multi-million dollar businesses do their first book. Sure, it was easier for them to launch a book than it was for us, since they had a list. But once again, if we can do it, it's possible – therefore, you can do it as well.

Another belief I've come across is, "Success as a writer is as likely as winning the lottery." Well, there are loads of authors out there who are supporting themselves solely from their writing. All you have to do is surround yourself with the proof that success is possible. Have a look at podcasts that go into the business of being a writer, like *The Creative Penn*, by Joanna Penn. Read books about the systems people use to write successful books. You'll soon see that once you have a repeatable system, which obviously doesn't exist in a lottery, becoming a successful writer is about following that system. You just have to work harder than the want-to-be writers, and stick to it until it works.

If you want to start, all you have to realize is that the only thing holding you back is your decision to start. As I mentioned in the *Introduction*, all you have to do is commit 100%. I'm not saying the process will be easy; however, you'll be one step ahead of everyone who didn't commit 100%. You'll avoid that ill-fated mental battle that requires willpower. Therefore, you will succeed at writing your book.

Mind Hack #2:

Read Around

"If you only read the books that everyone else is reading, you can only think what everyone else is thinking."
Haruki Murakami (Writer)

One of the biggest things you can do as an author is to read. Chances are if you're an author, or want to become one, you fell in love with reading a long time ago. I know I did. However, now that you're writing, you need to make this a regular activity that, short of an act of God, you never miss out on doing.

Reading has always been the most suggested way to improve as a writer. Plus, if you've ever struggled for ideas, reading something another writer has written is a surefire way to inspire yourself. The question is, though, what do you read?

To become a great nonfiction author there are three categories of books you want to read. First, you really need to read around on your subject. Partly because it lets you see what's out there, and partly because you need to know what other books in your field are saying and not saying.

Second, you need to read around in general for complementary topics, because that will broaden the way you can present your topic. Reading around in other completely different fields can be incredibly helpful too, because that is where you can learn about different styles of writing and different types of books. Some of those styles and book types might be new to you and suit your voice really well. Some might be what your audience responds to the best. So you end up becoming a better writer in the long run.

Finally, read fiction. Fiction writers are the experts on storytelling, and a large part of teaching in nonfiction is being able to tell stories well, so study your favorite fiction books. When you discover a scene you love, take it apart, word by word. Work out what made it so great, why you felt what you felt, how it captured your attention so you entered the world in the book and shut out everything else.

If you're a fiction writer, then read 'the greats' like Charles Dickens, read around in your genre and read other genres as well. Then read the nonfiction books that will help you research the background for your novels. So if you write crime novels, read about the police force. You get the idea. Read. And read some more.

A huge part of becoming a better writer is accomplished by reading well-written books and looking at how they were written. What did the author do to move you and what (in your opinion) made it a good book? Like any other occupation, though, you also want to read some really poorly written books so you can break them down and know what you have to avoid in your writing. Work out for yourself how they were written. What did the author miss that resulted in you staying at a surface level instead of getting into the book? Also, what jarred you and made you realize the book was poorly written?

When you train to become a copywriter, one of the first exercises all the teachers will make you do is to handwrite various top converting sales letters. This act lets them sink into your subconscious and allows you to see the patterns, phrasing, pace, and tone of the ones that work. If you apply this same exercise to all types of writing, you will quickly work out what it is about an author's style that worked for you as a reader. That then gets translated directly into your writing style and helps you improve even faster as a writer.

Just so you know, all the exercises are repeated at the back of the book, in case you want to read the whole book before doing the exercises.

Exercise: Read Around

Get hold of a book from an author you like. It doesn't need to have anything to do with your topic, you just have to find a style of writing you like and a book you got a lot from when you read it.

Spend an hour copying out some of your favorite sections, using whatever method you use to write your own material. So if you write by hand, copy these out by hand.

How does the author talk to the reader? How long are the sentences? If it's nonfiction, do they include exercises? If so, how much work is involved in the exercises? You want to dissect their writing as much as you can, because that is what's going to help you become a better writer.

Mind Hack #3:

Travel With a Map

*"Give me a store clerk with a goal and I'll
give you a man who will make history.
Give me a man with no goals and
I'll give you a store clerk."*

*James Cash Penny Jr
(Ex-Store Clerk, Founder of JC Penny)*

You know the old saying, "If you don't know where you're going, how will you know when you get there?" Well, the same goes for writing a book. You need to know your end goal. Now the obvious answer is, "When I have a book," probably followed by a few choice words. However, the book itself is rarely the end goal, especially not if you want to create a business from it, or use it to expand your current business.

You need to take some time, sit down, and work out what it is that you want to achieve so you'll know when you've succeeded. What's your end goal? To give you some inspiration, I've listed a variety of end goals from other authors, including:

1. To get new leads into my business
2. To improve my authority so I can get interviewed more
3. To see my book for sale
4. To see the look on a child's face when they read it
5. To help others change their lives

Some of these are well-structured end goals and some aren't. What I mean by that is if you look at #3, it's an end goal you can achieve without relying on someone else to do something. When you press publish and go to your book's page on Amazon, you'll see your book for sale. If that's your end goal, you'll know when you've achieved it.

However, if we look at an end goal like #5, how do you know when you've achieved it? Is it just one person's life you have to change, or more than that? How do you define change? A change for one person might be small, and that same change for a different person might be huge. So when you're defining your end goal, you need to define it in such a way that you'll know you've achieved it when it happens.

Another thing you need to consider when creating your end goal is the effect it has on the rest of your mindset. To avoid struggling with the belief that, "Writing might not pay off for me," you have to ensure that your end goal is something where you and only you are contributing to the outcome.

For instance, for #2, "To improve my authority so I can get interviewed more," you can do everything in your power to get yourself in the position to be interviewed, but it still depends on whether someone wants to interview you. Maybe your book positions you in the perfect way, but you live in an area where the internet is slow and you keep disconnecting, which leads to a dreadful interview. Does that mean your book failed? Of course not. If that was your end goal for your book, though, you can end up creating some mindset issues around writing. So make sure your end goal for your book is something where you are 100% in control of the outcome.

So what does your success map look like? How will you know you got there? One of the most powerful things you can do is share that goal with others. We've created the Bookthority Facebook group. It's for people like you who've read this book, which makes it a perfect place to share your goals. You can find out how to join in the *Conclusion*.

Mind Hack #4:

5-6-7 Why

"To succeed, you need to find something to hold on to, something to motivate you, something to inspire you."

Tony Dorsett (Football Running Back)

I'm sure you've heard people say that you need to focus on why you want something to help you stay motivated. It's true, your 'why' is a huge part of what will keep you going and pick you up in the tough times. However, as with most things, a subconscious reason lies behind your conscious answer. That's what we call your '5-6-7 Why'. That subconscious reason is going to speak to you on a much, much deeper level than any 'why' statement you've written out before.

We need to take some time and work out why you want to write a book, or continue writing if you've already started. There are several reasons for this.

First, writing a book isn't always easy. It does, however, become much easier if you have a big meaningful 'why'. Your reason will drive you when you're struggling to sit down and write because the kids want to come play, your clients want to talk to you, and your partner has barely seen you all week. Knowing the reason why you're sacrificing everything, and knowing it's worth the sacrifice, will keep you writing.

Second, having your 'why' can help you plan out your book's content. If the reason you want a book is to drive traffic to your business, then your book has to be relevant to your business. Not only that, it also has to be a topic that can stand alone, while complementing your business enough that it naturally drives your readers to your business for the next step.

Lastly, your 'why' will help you define the structure of your book. If you want to use your book to establish authority in your market, then you need to structure it in a way that shows off your authority. You'll naturally get authority just from being an author. To go to that next level, though, you need to give your readers the impression they are reading something professional. Use references to back up your data, just like you would if you wanted to write for an industry journal. And hire a good editor before it gets launched, because nothing will destroy your credibility faster than a poorly written book.

Your reason needs to be even bigger than that, though. Yes, you need the basic level of 'why' as well, since it will help you with various decisions along the way; however, you also need to find your '5-6-7 Why'. This is your reason from your deepest subconscious. This is what will speak to your reader through your writing and touch them at a much deeper level. It's what will create a longer-term successful book, and a movement that readers want to be part of. It's also what will help you know when you've succeeded. So how do you go about finding your '5-6-7 Why'? This technique comes from a true master of linguistics, Joe Stumpf.

Exercise: 5-6-7 Why

Take a piece of paper and write down a vertical list of the numbers one through seven.

Now ask yourself, "What's important to me about having a book?" / "What's important to me about being an author?" / "What's important to me about being a writer?" (Use whichever question resonates with you best.)

Write your answer next to number one.

Next, you're going to take the answer you just wrote out and ask yourself, "What's important to me about (your answer)?" And you want to write out that answer in the second slot.

Keep going all the way down to the seventh line.

To help you see this more clearly, here's an example:

"What's important to me about having a book?"

1. It will help me prove my credibility in my field.

    "What's important to me about proving my credibility in my field?"

2. It will help build my business.

    "What's important to me about building my business?"

3. I'll be able to help more people and earn money.

    "What's important to me about helping more people and earning money?"

4. I'll be less stressed and able to help people even more.

    "What's important to me about being less stressed and being able to help people even more?"

5. I'll be able to fulfill my purpose.

    "What's important to me about fulfilling my purpose?"

6. Others will get to fulfill their purpose.

    "What's important to me about others fulfilling their purpose?"

7. The world will become a better place.

As you can see, the further you go down into your subconscious reasons for doing things, the less it becomes about you, your ego, and your need for survival, and the more it becomes about others and the bigger picture.

The last three answers are your '5-6-7 Why', the reason you truly want to create your book. So write down, "I want to write a book because," and put in your '5-6-7 Why'. Then stick that up on your wall so you can see it whenever you write.

If you'd like to listen to an example of this, you can get an MP3 recording of me guiding my accountability partner through the process at 47MindHacks.com/567.

Mind Hack #5:

Set and Achieve Your Goals

*"A person who values their goals
actually values their achievements."*
Onyi Anyado (Speaker, Entrepreneur)

There have been more books than anyone could ever read on goal setting, so why include this chapter? Simple. The purpose of this book is to help you take action to change your mindset and, therefore, your results. While there's tons of information on goal setting, very little of it shows you what to do with your goals once you've set them. Hence why people rarely achieve their New Year's goals, or any other goals for that matter. So this chapter is about showing you exactly what you need to do with your goals, step by step, so you achieve them for a change.

The first step is to write out your goals. No, I'm not going to go into all the 'SMART' goal stuff. I've never had that work for me, any more than most others have.

What you want to do is write out exactly what you aim to achieve in the next twelve months. Yes, be specific, I'll give the SMART system that one. Saying you want to make more money is a goal you can achieve by walking outside and picking up a penny. So be specific.

I'm going to use the goal of writing a 60,000-word book as an example as we work through this so you can see the system in action. Now, if that time frame is too long, then feel free to shorten the time line. For the purposes of this example, though, we're going to stick with a twelve-month goal.

First off, you want to take your goal and break it down into smaller goals. That is what you need to achieve month by month to get to your end goal. For this example, that means writing 5,000 words a month. Next, take your monthly goals and break them into weekly goals. That ensures you reach your monthly end goal. Plan for a four-week month to keep things simple. For this example, that means you need to write 1,250 words per week. Finally, take those weekly goals and cut them down into five daily goals. That's 250 words a day for the example.

Breaking down a goal that way makes it far less daunting. You can imagine yourself writing just 250 words each day a lot easier than you can imagine yourself writing a whole book. What if you wanted to have it finished faster, though? Let's say you wanted to write your 60,000-word book in one month. What would the goal breakdown for that look like?

- 1 month = 60,000 words
- 1 week = 15,000 words
- 1 day = 3,000 words

You can see precisely what you need to achieve each day to stay on track. If you stick to that mini goal each day, then by the end of your twelve months (or your time frame), you will have achieved it. So, now you've seen the daily commitment, the questions you want to ask yourself are, "Do I still want to achieve that goal? And do I want to achieve it in the time line I picked?"

This is where your '5-6-7 Why' from the previous chapter comes into play. You want to create one for each of your big twelve-month goals. That is what is going to keep you going two months in when the end goal is still a long way off.

As you can see, if you truly want to achieve a goal, breaking it down into small daily chunks of actions can ensure your success. So there's really no reason now to miss achieving a goal. You simply have to want to achieve it and keep on track with your daily goals.

What I do to ensure I complete each of my daily goals is writing them into a spreadsheet where I keep all my daily and weekly goals, which stays open on my computer 24/7. Then, each day I write 'Win' next to my goal after I've completed it.

At the end of each week, I get together with my mastermind group who can see my goals checklist and whether I've completed everything.

I know I'll have someone to answer to at the end of the week if I miss any.

That way, if something happens that is out of your control (act of God, etc.), the worst-case scenario is you get a week behind on your goals. If that's the case, simply readjust your remaining monthly and daily goals to absorb the extra and get back to checking off your daily goal each day.

So what do you need to do today, to take that first step towards your goals?

Mind Hack #6:

The Power of Thought

"Thinking: the talking of the soul with itself."

Plato (Philosopher)

Have you ever noticed that when you're looking at buying a new car, the make and model you're considering seems to be everywhere? Or when you or your partner get pregnant, suddenly it seems like every woman in your town is pregnant? It's because by thinking a lot about those things, you've told your subconscious they're important to you so it makes sure you notice them when they're around you.

Let's try an experiment. Look around the room you're currently in for a blue object. They all jumped into your attention suddenly, right? Just thinking about blue objects is enough to get your subconscious primed to bring them to your attention.

You see, the way your subconscious works is by helping you get more of what you concentrate on and think about. I'm sure you've heard the saying before, "What you focus on expands." When you think about what you want, your subconscious will start working towards getting it for you. The key is to stay focused on one thing at a time, rather than flitting between different ideas and making your subconscious continually restart its work.

What does that mean for your success as a writer? If you focus on writing, finishing, or selling copies of your book, whatever stage you're at, then your subconscious is going to start bringing more of that to your awareness, including ways to help you achieve it.

The kicker is, your subconscious is completely unable to process a negative, or the word 'not'. If I say, "Don't think of how your hands feel," you instantly start thinking about your hands and how they feel. Why? Because exactly like those blue objects in your room, you just primed your subconscious to focus on how your hands feel. The 'not' of the word 'Don't' was completely ignored by your subconscious mind.

Same goes for when you're wanting to achieve something. If you start thinking about what you want to achieve, then everything works great. However, if you start thinking about what you want to avoid, you run into that problem of negatives again. The subject of the thought is the thing you want to avoid, so that's what your subconscious is focused on. That means you'll end up creating more of it because you just told your subconscious to focus on it.

Say you ultimately want to sit down and write every day. If you think about writing every day, your subconscious is focused on writing and will do everything in its power to help you write every day. If, however, you think about not missing a day of writing, then your subconscious is focused on missing a day of writing, and that's the result it will do its best to help you achieve. I know it's a fine line, but it makes all the difference to your results.

Mind Hack #7:

No One Is an Island

*"Success in any field, but especially
in business, is about working with
people, not against them."*
Keith Ferrazzi (Author)

Wouldn't it be great if a bunch of people, including some influencers in your field, all promoted your book when you launched? I can tell you from firsthand experience, it's an awesome feeling. So how do you get to that? Well, it's about having a network. As one of my mentors frequently says, "You want to build your network and create relationships before you need them."

The very last thing you're going to want to do is to finish your book, hit publish, then start contacting people about getting the word out. It's never going to happen that way. Not even the big names in your field, with all their contacts, do it that way. You have to start setting up your network and creating relationships as early as you can. The way to do it is to offer value to them. See how you can help them.

If you haven't read *Never Eat Alone* by Keith Ferrazzi, it's the best book out there on building a network. I'll let him go into all the details of how to do it and we'll just look at the mindset for it here.

Look at networking like a favor. When you do a favor for one of your close friends, do you expect them to immediately return the favor? Of course not. You have a relationship. You plan on staying friends forever. If they need help, you help them because you're friends. That's the way you want to look at building a business relationship. Rather than the usual attitude of, "What can you do for me right now?", just give without expecting anything in return; otherwise, the gift will feel like it has strings attached. So instead of feeling grateful and amazed, the recipient will feel like they have a stone around their neck.

Part of being able to set up a network of contacts is about having an abundant mindset. If you believe you are in competition with people, that will come across as you speak to people. It will almost certainly have an effect on how willing you are to help them, as well as on how you ask for their help. To put it simply, you have to go out and be prepared to just help them, without thinking about whether you're getting anything in return.

A quick way to go about creating a network is to promote other people's businesses. Mention them on your blog or inside your book, and let them know about it.

All of us only have 24 hours in a day. If you interact with your clients in any way, you can only help a limited number of them in a given time period. Chances are, there are way more people out there wanting what you do than you can possibly help in your lifetime. The same goes for your 'competition'. Basically, the pie is big enough for everyone. So instead of looking at them as competition, look at them as travelers on a similar journey and work out how you can help each other.

Another thing to remember is that some people are going to like you and some aren't. As long as you're in business to help people, rather than solely for the money, then you can still help the ones that don't gel with you, by recommending someone else they can work with.

Mind Hack #8:

Abundance Outlook

"Abundance is, in large part, an attitude."
Sue Patton Thoele (Author)

Deep down, everybody on the planet thinks they are a good person. Nobody thinks they're fundamentally bad or wrong. No, not even the people the press loves to hate. This belief in the fact that you're good will hold true no matter what goals you set for yourself. While that may sound like a good thing, it also affects the goals you can achieve.

Right about now, you might be thinking, "Well, that's fine. I don't want to do anything horrible, so this really doesn't affect me." Unfortunately, though, there's a good chance it does.

Let's say you want to succeed as a writer and make a living from it. However, you believe, "Rich people are evil," and despise what they stand for. The trouble is, if you want to make a living from your writing, you have to earn money. Money is the one thing that makes a rich person rich. Since you aren't evil and can never become something you despise or think is bad, your subconscious will do everything in its power to stop you earning money. When it comes to your subconscious, there is no gray, there's only black and white. While you might be able to differentiate between 'enough money to live on' and what you consider 'rich', your subconscious cannot. Money is money and having it is what you see as the cause of evil. Therefore, since you are good, you need to avoid it. So how do you solve this problem?

Well, the first step is to work out if it is a problem. What happens when you see other people having success or making money? What do you start thinking? Be completely honest here – after all, you're the only one who's going to know. If you're genuinely 100% happy about their success, then your subconscious will work towards helping you become successful too. If, however, seeing someone else succeed makes you jealous and think they didn't deserve it, then your subconscious will do its best to steer you away from becoming successful. Since you are a good person, you should only get what you do deserve, and you've just told your subconscious that success only comes to the undeserving. Starting to see the pattern here?

What it all comes down to for an abundant outlook is this: you need to admire the results and traits in others that you want to have yourself. This is what will get your subconscious and its considerable power to work towards getting you what you consciously want. So when someone you know succeeds, be happy for them. Look at all the work they did to get there and admire their persistence. If you're in a position to do something to help someone succeed, do it. There's room for everyone. The more you surround yourself with success, admire it, and focus on it, the faster you'll get there.

Mind Hack #9:

Don't Play the Blame Game

"Weak people never admit that they are responsible for their own state. They always blame either circumstances or others."

Amish Tripathi (Author)

We've all met those people who complain about everything. They're miserable to be around. Nothing ever seems to go their way and the entire universe is conspiring against them. At least as far as they tell it. Sadly, unless they change their behavior, they'll never change the things they're complaining about either. It's the catch 22 problem we looked at in the chapter *The Power of Thought*. They get what they focus on, which is the stuff they're complaining about.

However, when it comes to your results, there's actually another reason you want to avoid complaining and blaming something outside of yourself. It comes down to the fact that you can only change something you have control over. If you blame something outside of yourself, you're basically telling your subconscious that you don't have control over that result. And therefore, you don't have the power to change it.

By taking responsibility for your current results and situation, you're sending a clear message to your subconscious that you are in control and, therefore, you have the power to change the end result.

For example, you arrive late for a meeting and someone says, "What happened?" If you blame something you have no control over, for instance, "The traffic was dreadful," then you're telling your subconscious that it's okay to be late and it's not your responsibility.

Instead, if you said, "I left too late to get here in rush hour," you end up empowering your subconscious to avoid the same mistake next time. It's a subtle difference, but one that will change the end results you get in the long run. By claiming responsibility for the result, you take control and give yourself the chance to change your results.

Mind Hack #10:

Fail Fast

"Try again. Fail again. Fail better."
Samuel Beckett (Author)

How would it feel if, when you sat down to write, you already knew you had a long line of people who were waiting to buy your book? How motivated would you be to write it? I'd personally write like I had a fire under me.

One of the biggest fears I've found talking to various authors is the fear that, "No one will want my book when I've finished writing it." If you could have a bunch of people waiting for it, that would bust that fear.

The first step to avoid this outcome is to ask your intended audience before you start writing the book. That way you can get confirmation that you have a great idea for a book.

Of course, what happens if you put the idea for your book out there and all you get back are crickets, showing you there's zero interest? Well, in that case, I'd say congratulations. That's another great outcome. You see, you haven't wasted any time or money writing the book. You haven't spent months slaving away at it and making a deep connection with it, so you're not yet attached to the idea of it either. Being told there's no market for your book before you write it is perfect. Now you simply don't write it. That is what I mean by 'fail fast'.

It was the idea for the book that failed, rather than your actual book, since that doesn't exist yet. It was fast and, therefore, it saved you a huge amount of time and money, allowing you to quickly move on to the next idea with no feelings of regret. It's the same with the business you build off the back end of your books. You want to fail fast there too. If you have an idea for a course your readers might want, sell the idea first. Get people to put their money where their mouth is, and prove the idea is worth your time and effort to invest in it before you create it.

I realize this is the opposite way most people think of doing things with a book or a business. However, this is the way that will propel you toward success much faster. It'll also save you a lot of time and money, and keep you sane and somewhat relaxed throughout the process.

So what happens if you've already written the book? Or created the backend course? You've done every promotional tactic you can think of already: interviews, ads, guest posting, PR, and so on. Yet the book stubbornly refuses to sell. What do you do?

If you've genuinely done everything you can, even the stuff outside your comfort zone, and it hasn't moved the needle for you, then now is the time to move on. You want to go with the fail fast mentality. Rather than flogging a dead horse, sit down and examine it to work out why it failed. There's no point in beating yourself up about it, or stressing over it. It's the idea that failed to take off, not you. Your job now is to work out why that happened. That is what is going to make the time you spent writing it worthwhile. Think of that book as a paid course you took on how to avoid whatever mistake you uncover.

Once you've worked out what the mistake was, it's time for the next book. This time, though, you're going to test the idea before you start writing so you can fail fast with just the idea instead.

Want to know how to get people to tell you whether they'd buy your book before you've written it? Download a PDF guide to show you what to do at 47MindHacks.com/b4.

Dealing With the Inner Critic

*"Believe in yourself. Have faith in your
abilities. Without a humble but reasonable
confidence in your own powers you
cannot be successful or happy."*
Norman Vincent Peale (Author)

About ten years ago, after I'd had a rather bad day, my mentor at the time told me, "If one day you meet a jerk, oh well, big deal, you met a jerk – move on. However, if one day *everyone* you meet is a jerk, then you're the jerk."

Now before you close the book and start swearing at me, let me explain what that means in terms of how your mind works. You are bombarded with a ton of information – something like two million unique bits of information a second. If you tried to get your conscious mind to process it all, you'd go crazy. Even just the signals your body sends you, like "I need more oxygen, take a breath," would leave you no time for anything except keeping your body functioning. So your subconscious is left to do almost all the work. However, to do it effectively, it needs to have some systems in place.

Therefore, your subconscious sorts through all the information that comes at you. It gets filtered through your beliefs, values, and world view. Anything that doesn't fit simply gets ignored. Then it distorts and generalizes the rest until you're left with just seven items, which is all your conscious mind can handle each second. Needless to say, the end result is an extremely skewed version of reality.

Since everyone is unique, we all have slightly different beliefs and views. Therefore, your seven pieces of information are unique to you.

Expand that over a length of time, like several minutes, and it explains why three eye witnesses to an event can each give you a completely different picture of what happened.

So what does that have to do with my mentor's saying? Everything. The process your subconscious goes through, ensures those seven pieces of information confirm your beliefs and world view. If you believe that people are generally nice and out to help you, then that's what will show up in your seven bits and that's what you'll experience. On the flip side, if you believe that everyone is out to get you and sabotage you, then that is what you'll experience.

The process doesn't just stop with what you experience, though. Your subconscious also makes sure you feel the right emotion for the situation and tells you how to behave in response. It's like a never-ending catch 22 circle. You believe something so your subconscious ensures you experience it so you can reaffirm the belief. Everything you believe is true (for you), so you experience more of it.

So how does that relate to your inner critic? Well, if you want to get control of that inner critic and turn it into an inner supporter, then you have to change your filters to allow a different seven pieces of information through. That will completely change what you experience, what you tell yourself, what you take note of out in the world (criticism, praise, or anything else), and, ultimately, your results. After all, like my mentor's saying implies, you are what you experience.

Mind Hack #11:

There Is No Failure, Only Feedback

"Your best teacher is your last mistake."

Ralph Nader (Activist)

Where do you think we'd be as a species if toddlers gave up on learning to walk after falling because they considered it a failure?

According to Carol Dweck in the book *Mindset*, we all have one of two mindsets: a Growth mindset or a Fixed mindset. Everyone starts out with a Growth mindset. That's why the scenario of giving up when we learn to walk has never happened. All toddlers are encouraged by their parents to see the fall as feedback and to try again.

A Growth mindset is where we don't associate our behavior with our identity, so a 'failure' simply becomes feedback about how not to do something. We can then happily try again using a different method. A Fixed mindset, however, is where we associate our behavior with our identity and a 'failure' takes on the new meaning of "I am a failure." That is what trips people up and makes them so scared of failing. You can swap between mindsets and develop a Growth mindset any time, though. Carol Dweck's book shows you how, if you want to change it for yourself.

When it comes to anything new in our lives, just like when we learned to walk, we're almost certainly not going to get it 100% right the first time. So why do we expect writing a book to be the exception?

If you struggle with 'failure', or worry about criticism, which a lot of people equate to failure, then you want to start looking at your book as an experiment. After all, one of the awesome features of self-publishing a digital book is that you can change it anytime you want.

So why not get it out there, see what results you get, and update the things that didn't go so well to improve your book? Sure, you still need to get your book into the best state you can before you publish; however, all books can be improved by feedback from their ideal readers. Could one section have been explained slightly better? Would an extra exercise have helped the reader more? For fiction books, could you write a novella in an alternate reality with an alternative ending? I, for one, would love to read different endings to several of my favorite fiction books, just to see what might have been.

You want to keep that same outlook in mind during the writing process. Some days are going to be better than others. On the days that didn't go so well, work out what went wrong and change your process so more days go better. Doesn't that sound a lot more fun than feeling lousy for missing a week of writing?

Every single thing you do has an outcome. Either you got what you wanted (success), or you got the feedback about what went wrong so you can do something different and correct the outcome next time ('failure'). There really is no failure, it's just feedback.

Mind Hack #12:

Firing the Inner Fraud

"I don't know whether every author feels it, but I think quite a lot do – that I am pretending to be something I am not, because, even nowadays, I do not quite feel as though I'm an author."

Agatha Christie (Author)

I'm sure at least once since you started writing you've thought to yourself, "Why would anyone listen to me?", "I don't know what I'm doing," or, "I'm a fraud." It's called the Impostor Syndrome.

Everyone who is putting themselves out there, from writers to entrepreneurs, goes through that at various times. It's probably not the first time you've experienced it and, unfortunately, it won't be the last. It's just part of the roller coaster we all go through when we put our creativity out into the world for others to see.

As you can see from the quote, even the greats, like Agatha Christie, experience this. Yet no one in their right mind would look at her and question whether she was actually an author.

The key to limiting how often you feel this way, is to have a system in place, before you need it, to pull you out of this self-doubt faster. That way you don't waste days, weeks, or months beating yourself up, feeling dreadful, and more importantly, not writing.

Eventually, everyone will pull themselves out of it and write. Your job right now is to work out what precisely got you out of it last time. Was it your spouse saying they believed in you? Was it some readers' 'thank you' letters that you read? Did you look at the positive reviews of your last book or testimonials from your business, and realize you are helping people? Whatever it was, this is going to be the start of your system.

Write out all the things that make you feel better when you're going through self-doubt, and put them in a document you can get your hands on from anywhere. I personally use Google Docs. To give you some inspiration, here's what my document says:

1. Tell Steve I feel unconfident and need some help.
2. Read Sarah's, Topher's, and Christa's Amazon reviews (for my previous book).
3. "This is a great book, you should be proud of it," – Topher (someone in the industry that I really respect).
4. "This is gold! I'd be interested in reading the rest when it's finished!" – test reader feedback for a section of this book.
5. Stand up straight.
6. Ground yourself.
7. Take four deep breaths and imagine the negativity coming out as black smoke every time you exhale.
8. Go for a walk on the beach.

Finally, when you need help from this information, look at the document and follow through with every single item on it. No thinking about it. No skipping steps. Simply read or take action on every single item as required. When you're back to feeling confident again, if some things on your list didn't help, cross them off. If you did extra things that did work, add them to the list. You want this system to change as you change.

This document will help you pick yourself up extremely fast if you use it as soon as you start feeling like an impostor. The less time you can spend in the dips of the writer's and entrepreneur's roller coaster, the faster you'll become successful.

Exercise: Firing the Inner Fraud

Create a document you can easily find from anywhere. I personally use Google Docs. Write out all the things you need to do to pick yourself up when you're going through self-doubt.

Mind Hack #13:

Down With Perfectionism

"Perfectionism is not a quest for the best. It is a pursuit of the worst in ourselves, the part that tells us that nothing we do will ever be good enough – that we should try again."

Julia Cameron (Author)

While doing my research, I came across the belief, "I struggle to know when the book is ready." That partly comes from not having a system in place, without which you don't know what your milestones are and what your editing process is. The other part is that you want your book to be perfect.

There's a lot of different advice available on how to write, what to do for the editing phases, and how to publish. Since this is a book on mindset, I'm going to leave the 'how to' to other books, courses, and information out there. You want to find a process that works for you and go with it. We're going to focus solely on the struggle with perfectionism.

The first step is to define what makes a book 'perfect'. A lot of writers and other creatives struggle with things being perfect because they define it as being exactly what they envisioned when they started writing. That might be no mistakes, brilliantly written clever phrases, witty anecdotes, and a perfect flow from chapter to chapter.

Let's face it, even with several editors, proofreaders, beta readers, and yourself combing through your book, there's always a couple of little typos that somehow make it through. It happens to books published by the Big Five too, it's not just a self-publishing issue. Your readers aren't reading your book for the lack of mistakes; they're reading it for the information or the story. As long as it's been edited, the odd typo isn't going to affect the success of your book and can easily be corrected at a later date.

For a nonfiction book, the danger comes when 'perfect' gets defined as 'perfect as far as the author is concerned'. That's because 'perfect' for you, as the author, isn't necessarily the same as 'perfect' for your readers. If you've ever asked your fan base for feedback on potential covers, or to vote on different titles for your book, you will have discovered that the 'surefire winner' you thought they'd pick, isn't always the winner. Sometimes the winner even ends up being an extra choice you threw in there at the last minute just to provide another option. Instead, you need to define 'perfect' as something that will help your reader solve their problem.

What that essentially means, is that until you have reader feedback, you can't tell if the book is 'perfect'. So you have to be open to letting others read it while you're still in that unsure phase, and then tweaking it once you have their feedback.

For fiction books, 'perfect' can involve your long-term fan base. What character do they want to know more about? Who do they wish would get together? What leader are they hoping will win the upcoming battle? This can work even for new authors. There are writers putting their books out chapter by chapter online. Their readers provide feedback about what they like and what they don't like. Towards the end you can get a few beta readers involved in working out what they think will happen, what they'd like to see happen, and what they'd hate to see happen. That will help you shape the ending so it comes as a bit of surprise, yet doesn't disappoint them.

Basically, it all comes down to the purpose of your book. Is the purpose getting your readers to learn something? Is it to bring new clients into your business? Is it to give your readers a break from reality and let them engage with their imagination, like magic and fantasy books do for me? If your purpose is for you to check 'writing a book' off your bucket list, and you don't care if anyone ever reads it, then you don't need reader feedback. However, if your purpose is anything other than that, then you're going to have to involve your readers. Their opinions are what's going to get you to fulfill the purpose of your book.

So if you want your book to be 'perfect', the rather counterintuitive first step is to let go, give it to your readers, and see what they say. Does it fulfill the purpose it was created for? If so, congratulations! Despite any errors, you have created what you set out to create. Errors can be corrected. If, however, it doesn't fulfill its purpose, the feedback should tell you what needs to be changed so the next version of the book will be infinitely closer to being 'perfect'.

Mind Hack #14:

I'm Not Good Enough

"The only way to be a novelist, to think
that you can create something others will
give themselves up to for a dozen hours
or more, is to have psychotic self-belief."

Nicola Griffith (Author)

A belief I've come across a number of times in my research is, "I'm not good enough to be a writer." If you have this limiting belief, what I'd like to ask you is, "Not good enough compared to what / whom?"

You see, most "I'm not … enough" beliefs stem from comparing ourselves to others. Just becoming aware of that comparison is often all it takes to make you realize just how silly it is.

For instance, "I'm not good enough… compared to Jane Austen." Well, how long did it take her to become the writer that wrote *Pride and Prejudice*? I seriously doubt that was her first attempt at writing anything. The same applies to pretty much any famous author out there. Whether they started writing blog posts, short stories, research papers, articles, or anything else, what you're seeing is them after they've put in a lot of hard work.

As the saying goes, "The reason you struggle with insecurity is because you compare your 'behind the scenes' with everyone else's 'highlight reel'."

So how do you break out of this trap, if you're not already laughing at your comparisons now? One of the things I've learned in my studies is that if one person can do something, all you have to do is work out their system for doing it, and then use the system yourself to create similar results. We already know there are numerous good writers out there. Therefore, it's possible to become a good writer. I'm not saying it won't take work, but as long as it's possible you can achieve it as well if you put your mind to it.

Your actual writing skills, as with anything, will continue to improve the more you practice. No one, not even the greats, wrote a classic the first time they put pen to paper. If you've never done any writing training, buy a book or three from Amazon on how to write. Make sure you buy a fiction book that relates to your genre, or a specific nonfiction book if you're going that route. The process differs widely and you want to follow the one that works. Once you've learned a system, practice, practice, practice. The more you write, the faster you'll improve.

At some point in the future, you will look back at the stuff you're writing now and realize just how much you've improved. However, for now, you're good enough to start writing. Learn from the feedback and improve. No one starts out being awesome and unless you start, you have nowhere to improve from.

Mind Hack #15:

I Now Pronounce You Worthy

"Self-worth comes from one thing –
thinking that you are worthy."

Wayne Dyer (Author)

"I'm not going to set up a meeting with this influential person who might be able to help me, because why would THEY want to meet ME?" When I read this belief a few days ago, I was floored. I thought I'd cleared all my limiting beliefs. Clearly not. This one had me thinking: good question, why would they? So this chapter is about what I did to clear it and pick my self-image back up off the floor.

If you're also thinking, "That's a good question, why would they want to meet me?", think about it this way: "Why wouldn't they want to meet you?" I don't know about you, but my answer was, "Because I have nothing I can offer them." Of course, Steve's reply was, "Yeah, absolutely nothing. After all, they grew up where you grew up. They had the exact experiences you've had. They've learned everything that you've learned, and they've spoken with everyone you've spoken to. That coupled with the fact that you are obviously omnipotent and know exactly what they're thinking about, what they're doing, and what they're wanting to know more about. So yeah, why would they want to meet you?"

What can I say, he's into tough love, but he's completely right. We're all a unique collection of our experiences and knowledge. Something you think is common knowledge they might not know. Someone you grew up with might be the exact person they're desperate to meet. Remember, it doesn't have to be knowledge or people in their industry.

For instance, if you're both in the field of finances, they might have a child that is struggling with continuous ear infections, and because your best friend is a chiropractor, you know how to help them. The possibilities are endless.

Rather than assume they wouldn't want to meet you, flip it on its head and ask yourself, "What if I knew the one thing they most needed, and I let my narrow thinking and insecurity stop me from meeting them? How would I feel?" The answer for me would be pretty dreadful. So I'll ask you again, "Why would they want to meet you?" Hopefully you're now thinking, "Hmm, good question. Why wouldn't they want to meet me?"

Mind Hack #16:

Picking Up the Pieces

"We're our own dragons as well as
our own heroes, and we have to
rescue ourselves from ourselves."
Tony Robbins (Motivational Speaker)

When everything goes wrong and the writing habit you carefully set up falls apart, how do you get back on the horse again? We've all been there. Sometimes, as they say, "Life happens." Maybe it was a family emergency, or you got laid off from your job, or whatever. At the end of the time out, you need to be able to pick yourself up, dust yourself off, and get back to writing. So how do you do that?

The best way is to have a system, designed before you need it, that you can just implement without worrying about it. Step by step. I call this your 'Pick Up Plan'.

So what does this system need to have?

1. It needs to make you remember why you want to write.
2. It needs to be incredibly quick to execute and so easy you can't possibly fail.
3. It needs to have an increasing word count goal built into it to get you back to your original daily habit.

You essentially want to get yourself to do some writing, however little, just to remind your subconscious that you're back to writing and you are a writer. For this we're going to follow the habit formation method of *trigger, action, reward* from the Stanford professor BJ Fogg. A trigger is something that occurs in your life every day, around the same sort of time. For example, your alarm clock going off every morning. The action is what you want to do every time the trigger happens. In this case, sit down and write. And finally, the reward is something you want, and get as a result of completing the action.

You want to design your rescue system around a trigger that you still have in place, despite the situation that put the brakes on your writing. This could be your alarm clock going off in the morning, or sitting at your desk first thing. You preferably want to use the same trigger you used before so the transition back to your old habit is easier.

When this trigger occurs, the first thing you want to do is to read your '5-6-7 Why' statement that is the reason you write. You created it in the *5-6-7 Why* chapter. That gets you in touch with your true desire that you want to fulfill and will motivate you enough to start on this system.

Next, sit down to write for a really small length of time. Something really easy that you can manage even with what's going on. Something like five or ten minutes. Remember, the actual content of what you write is only half the result here. Just getting writing again is the other half. That tiny amount of time fulfills the 'quick and easy' part of the requirement.

Now you want to design a reward that will make you feel good. For me, it's putting a 'Win' next to my goal on my spreadsheet. Yes, I know, it's sad, but I get a huge kick from doing it, so it works for me. It doesn't have to be anything big, it just has to mean something to you personally. Preferably something that you'll regret missing out on if you miss the action, because if you don't complete it, you don't get the reward.

Finally, you want to create your escalation phase. This is where you increase your writing time by a little amount each day until you're back into your daily writing habit. The reason for this is it took you a while to set up your initial habit, so chances are just spending one day on your 'pick up plan' isn't going to get you back to where you were. So you want to take the small first step and increase it little by little until you feel you're back into your habit.

Go ahead and do the exercise below, and create your 'Pick Up Plan' before you need it.

You can get a copy of my pick up plan and a template to create your own at 47MindHacks.com/Pickup.

Exercise: Picking Up the Pieces

Write out your trigger, action, reward, and escalation for your pick up plan.

Trigger = Something that signals you to start the behavior, like your alarm clock.

Action = Write for a short time, like five minutes or ten minutes.

Reward = Something you want, that you only get if you complete the action step.

Escalation = How you're going to increase the action a little bit each day to get back to your original habit.

Mind Hack #17:

Butting Out Limiting Beliefs

"It is our interpretation of the past, our limiting beliefs, and our undigested pain that stop us from being able to move forward with clear direction."

Debbie Ford (Author)

One of the most powerful words in the English language is the word 'but'. Your subconscious mind processes this in a very unique way. What happens is that it disregards everything in the sentence before the word 'but' as false. It then replaces it in your belief system with everything that came after the word 'but'.

That technique has been used very cleverly by salesmen for years. They can say something that you believe to be true, then say 'but', and add something they prefer you to believe instead. For instance, "I know writing every day can be really difficult, but this system helps make it a reality." What your subconscious gets from that statement is, "This system helps make writing every day a reality." Anything that was placed before the word 'but' is completely ignored by your subconscious mind.

Rather than letting some random salesperson influence the way you think, it's time to take the power of the word 'but' and use it yourself to start changing the limiting beliefs your inner critic keeps voicing.

Let's look at how this works with a common belief that I heard from writers while doing my research. The belief of, "Nobody will want to read this."

I'm 100% certain you can find one person, somewhere in the world, that will want to read what you've written. Whether that's your best friend, your partner, or even your mother. There's someone out there that you can say will want to read it, even if no one else does. Right?

When you hear yourself think, "Nobody will want to read this," you want to add, "But someone will." The resulting statement is, "Nobody will want to read this, but someone will." What goes into your subconscious from this sentence is that "Someone will want to read this." Now, while that word is incredibly powerful, it's not going to change your belief right then and there. What it does do, though, is open your mind to the possibility that the belief might be wrong. If you keep repeating the new ending to your sentence every time you hear it, your mind slowly gets used to the fact that belief is false. That is when things like affirmations can start working, because you're now doubting the old belief, so your subconscious is open to changing it.

Anytime you come across your inner critic spouting a limiting belief, work out what one small thing goes against it. There are very few, if any, absolutes in this life. You want to look for the tiny exceptions your conscious mind can agree are true that are the opposites of your limiting belief.

Another example I heard a lot was the belief, "My content is crap and I'm kidding myself." So what is a tiny opposite for that? How about, "Some of it is good"? Or if that's too much, "One point I made is good." It doesn't matter how small the exception is, you just need to find it. This belief then becomes, "My content is crap and I'm kidding myself, but one point I made is good." Once again, you've proved to your subconscious that the absolute you started with is false, so it can ignore it and focus on the fact that some of your content is good.

I'll leave you with, "I know getting control of your inner critic can be difficult, but this system will help make it much easier."

Exercise: Butting Out Limiting Beliefs

Your subconscious disregards everything in the sentence before the word 'but' as false, and replaces it with everything that came after the word 'but'.

Find a limiting belief you want to change. Something like, "Nobody will want to read this," or, "My content is crap and I'm kidding myself."

Work out a tiny exception to it. Something like, "Someone will want to read it," or, "Some of it is good." It doesn't matter how small the exception is; just find one.

Combine the two sentences with a 'but' between them. For example, "Nobody will want to read this, but someone will."

Mind Hack #18:

Instant Self-Belief

*"If you want to be enthusiastic,
act enthusiastic."*

Dale Carnegie (Author)

Can you imagine what it would be like if every time your inner critic had a go at you, you could just flip and switch, and instantly gain back your self-confidence? No? Well by the end of this chapter, that's exactly what you'll know how to do.

Your subconscious mind is very much like a computer. You put data in and get a result out. If you put the same data in, you get the same result out. If you put different data in, you get a different result out. When it comes to your subconscious, the data is in the form of thoughts and emotions. The results you get out are what's called your 'state'.

Once your inner critic has had its go at you and you feel lousy, you're in a 'disempowered' state. To get back to feeling awesome about yourself and your writing, you have to move from a disempowered state to an 'empowered' state. The way to do that is to change the data going in.

One of the awesome features of your subconscious mind is that it is completely incapable of telling the difference between reality and a manufactured reality that you feed it. As long as it gets its data (thoughts and emotions), it responds by producing a result (your state).

So what we need is a way of manufacturing the reality you want. Or, as it says in the quote for this chapter, if you want to be enthusiastic, act enthusiastic. Your subconscious is incapable of telling the difference.

There are three steps to instantly change your state. By 'instantly' I do mean about five minutes, but considering it usually takes people hours to days, or sometimes even months, to pick themselves up and get back on the horse, I'm counting five minutes as 'instant'.

Step 1 – Change Your Posture

Your posture has been shown to affect your state and vice versa. As a quick example, try this. Sit in a chair and slouch. Really round that back, pull your shoulders forward, and drop them down. Bend your neck down until you're looking towards the floor. Turn the corners of your mouth down into a 'sad face'. Now, with a deep, quiet voice, slowly say, "I feel really motivated." Do you feel motivated? Of course not. You are more likely feeling lethargic, demotivated, and kind of lousy. If you didn't try this out, give it a go. You don't need to say the words out loud; you can just say them in your head.

Now, sit up, or better yet (if you can do it where you are), stand up. Sit or stand straight, like someone trying to make themselves look taller. Plant your feet hip width apart, with your weight evenly between them. Pull your shoulders back. Look straight ahead. Put a big smile on your face. Now, with a mid-range, loud voice, quickly say, "I feel really sad." Do you feel sad? Of course not. Instead, you probably feel determined, happy, and energized. If you're like me, you're probably laughing at how silly you sound saying you're sad.

That is how much posture can change your state. And that is the basis of an instant state change after your inner critic has had a go at you.

So, ask yourself, "How would a confident bestselling author stand?" Chances are they'd stand up straight, with their shoulders back. How else do you think a confident bestselling author would stand? For one minute, stand as if you were this bestselling author, confident in your success. It's okay to be an actor for a minute, after all you just did something similar above.

Step 2 – Change Your Breathing

Your breathing tends to be aligned with your posture, in that it's hard to take a deep breath if you're hunched over, or trying to make yourself small. It's equally very natural to take deeper, stronger breaths if you're standing up straight.

So, ask yourself, "How would a confident bestselling author breathe?" Chances are they'd take some nice deep breaths. Keep your posture from step one going for another minute, while you add in a few nice deep breaths, followed by some even, unrestricted breathing as if you were this bestselling author, confident in your success.

Step 3 – Change Your Self-Talk

If you remember, I said that the data going into your subconscious is your thoughts and emotions. Steps one and two took care of the emotions, so now it's time for the thoughts.

Ask yourself, "What would the self-talk of a confident bestselling author sound like as they thought about their books and their writing ability?" Once again, this time for three minutes, I want you to pretend you are this bestselling author. Keep the posture and the breathing going, and start mentally saying all the things you imagine a successful author would tell themselves. You want to hear yourself saying these things quite quickly, firmly, and with some power behind them, just like a confident person would.

I'll leave it to you to work out exactly what your idea of a bestselling author would say to themselves, because only you know what you need to overwrite your inner critic's negativity. For inspiration, my bestselling author says things like, "My readers love my books, leave lots of positive reviews, and recommend them to their friends. I find topics people are wanting books on and deliver great content. I easily write every day."

Emphasize the key words in this self-talk, to really bring out the certainty that a confident person would have. For my example, I emphasize, 'love', 'lots', 'recommend', 'great', and 'easily'.

At the end of this five-minute exercise, have a think about your new state. Do you feel empowered and confident again? If you've followed the exercise, then you'll have accomplished what I talked about at the start of this chapter. The ability to just flip and switch, and instantly gain back your self-confidence after your inner critic has had a go at you.

If you stay in your empowered state, by keeping your posture and breathing going, you should be able to think about what your inner critic said and realize how silly it sounded. Just like you did in the first exercise where you experimented with your posture and said the opposite of how you felt (the 'I feel really motivated' experiment).

Exercise: Instant Self-Belief

1. Ask yourself, "How would a confident bestselling author stand?" For one minute, stand like that. Stand up straight, with your shoulders back, and do anything else you think they would do.
2. Ask yourself, "How would a confident bestselling author breathe?" For one minute, keep the posture going and breathe like they would. Take a few deep breaths, then breathe as a bestselling author would.
3. Ask yourself, "What would a confident bestselling author sound like as they think about their books and their writing ability?" For a final three minutes, keep the posture and breathing going, and mentally tell yourself all the things you imagine they would tell themselves.

Standing Out

"You go to the airport and look at the bookstand and you feel the titles are similar, the covers are similar, and you wonder how they can be different."

Kenneth Branagh (Actor, Director)

To write a book that people will buy, you have to write something they want to read. Obvious, I know. But when you have a topic like writing faster or building a business, or something about which there are already multiple books, how do you get people to buy your particular book? Simple, you have to make yours stand out.

While the answer might be simple, the process of doing it isn't necessarily easy. There seem to be quite a few limiting beliefs that hold people back from successfully standing out. That is what this section is all about.

Mind Hack #19:

Embrace Your Uniqueness

"The things that make me different
are the things that make me."

A. A. Milne (Author)

When it comes to standing out, you want to embrace what makes you, you. That's the foundation of any good brand, and a brand is designed to help you stand out. Part of having a brand is consistency, so when people read all your books, they can see the same voice appearing across all of them. It's what makes people read everything you have written. In nonfiction, it's the fact that they like your voice, your topic, how you teach, and your quality of information. In fiction, it's the fact that they like your voice, your genre, your characters, and your stories.

I've previously struggled with the belief, "Why would anyone want to read what I write, when it's a well-covered topic?" I used to think that since there was already a book on a topic, I should avoid writing about it. However, I've since come to realize that was a limiting belief and I was doing my potential readers a disservice by thinking that way.

With nonfiction, chances are the topic you're covering isn't completely new, unless you're a researcher on the very edge of your field. Topics like productivity, writing habits, time management, and others have all been written about countless times before. So what makes a book by you, on that topic, stand out? It's your unique process. The way you approach it, what you think about when you're solving the problem, and your personal story of how solving the problem changed your life are all things a reader wants to know about. They might have read numerous books on the topic, and still their problem remains unsolved, because no one has expressed the solution in precisely the way they need to hear it. For your audience, that is what your book will give them. That's why they're your audience.

You want to embrace your unique way of looking at the problem. Stop worrying that the topic isn't a new one and you're not the first person to address it. Maybe that one little thing you've added to your process is exactly what your readers need to hear to make the solution work for them.

When it comes to fiction, you can tell from the first few lines of a book whether you want to read the rest. With an author you like, you know their voice will be consistent across all their books. That way you know you're going to like the book without having to read the first few paragraphs. That is what I mean by embracing your uniqueness when it comes to fiction. Sure, the story is going to be unique, but your reader also needs to be able to recognize your voice in every one of your books. There are several fiction authors that I love, and I buy everything they write. I never look at their books beforehand to work out if I want them. If they wrote it, I buy it, because I love their voice.

So embrace your voice and your unique perspective. Never try to sound like someone else, not even someone whose style you love. Be you. That is why people will read your books.

Mind Hack #20:

People Don't Know What You Know

*"Never assume that what is common
sense to you is known by everyone."*

Robert Abela (Website Security Expert)

I've often heard authors say, "I have nothing revolutionary to add to my topic. Why would anybody be interested in a book like that?"

We quite often have the habit of trivializing what we know really well. After all, it's obvious to us, so surely everyone else knows it too, don't they? The answer is a very resounding, "No, they don't." This is especially true when you've spent a lot of time working on the same topic. It's amazing how you forget what it felt like when you first started out. All the knowledge you now take for granted was something you initially didn't know and, more importantly, something your current ideal readers and clients still don't know.

A friend of mine, Robert, specializes in website security. He was writing away about all the new techniques for protecting your site, the new vulnerabilities that hackers were targeting, and all the super detailed high-level stuff that realistically only other security professionals like him would understand. The reason he did this was that, like most experts, he figured the basics were available for free all over the internet, so there was no point in him covering them. His breakthrough came when, after loads of reader questions about the basics, he put together some information on topics like, 'Why you need a strong password'. Needless to say, it was quite an epiphany for him. He's been putting all his knowledge into his writing ever since, much to the delight of his readers.

When it comes to how you process information, what's going on is that you, as an expert, already have the big picture in the back of your mind for how your information fits into the scheme of things. It's something you know so well you've forgotten you had to work it out, so you assume that everyone sees it. However, that's not the case. This missing context is why your readers are left having to ask the basic questions. Hearing about what's obvious to you will give your readers the chance to make sense of all the information they've been learning about your topic. It's going to give them that 'ah ha' moment they're looking for as all the pieces magically slot into place and their understanding of the topic dramatically increases.

The ultimate plus side of this is that they end up seeing you as even more of an expert now you've helped them organize their thoughts about your topic and shown them how all the information they have fits together.

If we go back to my friend Robert, he understands why hackers do what they do. At best, most people have a misguided idea about why a website gets hacked. They ask questions like, "Why do I need a strong password?", or, "Why would someone attack my site; I'm not selling anything?" Just sharing his knowledge of the context helps them understand website security at a much deeper level. Now they know what hackers are really looking for, they've moved on to ask better questions, like, "What constitutes a strong password?" They've stopped thinking that their site was irrelevant to hackers simply because they had an unimportant, small site with few readers, or they didn't sell anything.

That is the power of the information that's locked away in your mind. It doesn't have to be revolutionary to make a difference to your audience. The stuff you take for granted is probably what your readers really need to hear. So as you're writing, keep in mind people don't know what you know.

Mind Hack #21:

Competition Is Good

"Having no competition is a bad thing.
Competition makes you try to
improve yourself all the time."
Shu Qi (Actress)

A lot of people see competition as something scary. They think that if they can just find a topic no one else has covered yet, they'll do really well. I know I've been guilty of that particular belief in the past. However, given that books, or the businesses around them, are far from new inventions, the exact opposite is true.

Obviously, you don't want to write a very similar book to your competition, but providing you can work out a way that makes you stand out from the crowd, then competition on a topic is actually what you're looking for.

It's the same for books as it is for businesses. If someone (the pioneer) is making money, then inevitably a bunch of other books or businesses will pop up that do something very similar, because the first person proved there was a market for that topic.

Think about it: if you're interested in a topic, say writing, do you only buy a single book on it or follow a single influencer? Of course not. If you're like me, you probably buy several or even all of the long-term top books on the subject, plus some of the new ones at the top of the field. The ones that have proven themselves to sell well.

You're going to want to do this for your topic. That way you can learn from them, and work out if there is a gap anywhere in the market that you could write a book around. You can see whether there's a problem that no one currently seems to be solving.

On the other hand, if there are no good selling books on that topic, there are only two reasons that cause this.

1. It's a completely new topic. Something like a new diet, technology, toy, or game.
2. No one is looking for books on this topic.

If you luck out and it's the first reason, you can take a chance and write a book to see if a new market pops up around the new topic. It's risky and, as they say, "You can spot a pioneer by the arrows in their back." However, if you happen to prove the market, the next two to three people will likely end up being the ones that write the top selling books for that topic. They'll learn from your book what worked, and what the reviewers liked and didn't like, and they'll write their book with the new existing market in mind. So while being the first sounded good, being the second or third to market is much, much better and less risky.

If, however, it's the second reason, then you'll end up with a book that arrives in a blaze of glory from your launch, only to sink nearly as fast to the depths of the Amazon rankings because no one is looking for it, so you get zero organic traffic.

Ultimately, as I hope you now realize, competition in a market is a good thing. It's the biggest indicator of a good topic to write your book on, and it's the proverbial 'green' light instead of a 'red' one.

Mind Hack #22:

Your Book Is Not for Everyone

*"We know what happens to people
who stay in the middle of the road.
They get run down."*
Aneurin Bevan (Politician)

Your goal as a writer is to have as many readers as possible read your book and, if applicable, take action on it to change their lives in some way. If that isn't your goal, you should probably put this book down.

Nobody sets out to write a book that will die an unmissed death in the depths of Amazon. So what makes new books popular and what makes readers want to read them?

We could go into the details here with nice-looking covers, and catchy titles, and all that. However, I'm talking about a more generalized, fundamental reason. It's simple. New books get read because readers are looking for something that either solves a problem they have (nonfiction) or sounds interesting (fiction).

If there are already several bestselling books that solve a specific problem, then most readers won't look any further, unless either their solutions don't work or a new book promises to solve the problem in a different way. So how do you show your solution is different? One of the ways you can do that is to niche.

Fiction authors, for the most part, already have this figured out. They write to a genre, which is a way of niching.

Nonfiction authors, however, still seem to think that reaching the largest audience possible is the best thing they can do. Unfortunately, though, you can't write a book for 'everyone'. It's the fastest way to get your book to become obscure. Instead, you want to tailor your book to a group of people so that it really speaks to them and repels everyone else.

Let's say there are five books on habits that sell well. If your expertise is around creating habits and you want to write a book about that, then you have to make yours stand out somehow. One way to do that is to niche it for a specific group of people. Write a book on habits for authors or habits for entrepreneurs, you get the idea. That way your ideal reader will value your book over a bestselling general one, because it's more specific to them and, therefore, all the content should apply to their exact situation.

Yes, there are fewer people overall in the niche compared to 'anyone' looking for a book on your topic, but those people in your niche are much more likely to pick your book over the others when it comes time to buy.

Mind Hack #23:

Be the Purple Cow

"In a crowded marketplace, fitting in is failing. In a busy marketplace, not standing out is the same as being invisible."

Seth Godin (Author)

As Seth Godin says in his book *Purple Cow*, the same old, same old just gets forgotten because it's not worth talking about. However, if you're different, you're remarkable. To have any hope of success in a crowded market, you have to be remarkable.

Until people have read your book, they can only tell whether it is different from the others on that topic by looking at your title, cover, and book description. Unless your title and cover stand out enough, though, your book description never gets seen. So how do you go about making your title and cover stand out?

Well, it comes down to research. To be able to stand out, you have to know what you need to stand out from. For example, wearing bright orange might make you stand out in London, but if you're surrounded by a bunch of others wearing bright orange, you blend in once again. As Seth Godin says, in a field of cows a purple one stands out, but if purple becomes the new 'norm', then it ceases to stand out.

Once you know how everyone else has positioned themselves on the topic, you can start to work out where the gaps are and how your book can be different. One way to really stand out, is to approach your topic from a completely different perspective to all the other books. For instance, to stand out from all the 'write faster' books, you could create a book on why writing too fast becomes a problem and how to find your optimum speed instead.

Another way to stand out is to pick a smaller niche, like we examined in the previous chapter, *Your Book Is Not for Everyone*. You could also stand out with your type of book:

- Interview book
- List / tips book
- Step-by-step, in-depth guide
- Quick read – just the minimum you need to know on one specific problem
- A collection book – part of a series of highly specific books around a larger topic

You want to approach the puzzle of finding that gap from as many different directions as you can and see what you can come up with. Release yourself from the need to get it right with your first idea, and brainstorm as many different ways as you possibly can within a thirty-minute period. Don't edit your ideas. Don't second-guess whether they're any good. Simply write them down and move on.

When your time is up, read through your list. Which of them might work? Which go against what you believe? Which do you like and which do you hate? Make a short list and go from there. Pick your one perspective that will make you stand out and use it to create the purpose for your book. What is the one point of view that you need to get across with your book? That is what you want your readers to take away and remember, even a year after they've finished your book. If you've done this exercise well, that one thing will make your book stand out in your market.

Lastly, make sure that your title expresses this purpose so it shows clearly how your book stands out from the rest. Then use the cover to also express it so buyers can quickly see at a glance why your book is different.

Exercise: Be the Purple Cow

Write out what each book in your market focuses on and what (from the title and cover) you think the book is about.

Brainstorm for thirty minutes about ways and perspectives in which your book could be different so it stands out from what already exists.

Knock your list down to your short list by removing the ideas you don't like or don't believe in.

Finally, pick your one item and use it to define the purpose of your book.

Pick a title and cover that express this purpose.

Mind Hack #24:

Dare to Be Different

"Trying to get everyone to like you
is a sign of mediocrity."
Colin Powell (Military Leader)

In every field you have the top people, or influencers, and everyone else. The influencers all write and speak on their topic. If you don't already follow the ones in your field, that's something you'll want to do. One of the reasons is that to stand out from them and have your unique perspective, you need to know what you have to stand out from. There are plenty of other reasons, like staying on top of the latest information in your field, creating a network that you can cross-promote others with, and so on, but for the purposes of standing out, you simply need to know their positioning in the market so you can be different.

Every single influencer or top expert in any field has a way of standing out and being different. Sure, there might now be ten 'me too' authors, bloggers, or businesses who try and copy them, but they were unique when they started. Their uniqueness is a large part of why they rose to the top and it's the reason their tribe follows them. You see, no one follows a 'me too'. There's no point.

So make a list of the top books in your market, especially the long-term bestsellers, and write down what makes them different. Do they stand out by niching for a group of people, like 'time management for authors'? Do they stand out by the book length, like the short reads books? Do they stand out by book style, like an interview book or a comprehensive guide book?

Once you have the full list, it's time to get your mind around how you can stand out. Have a think about your ideal reader. What do they all have in common, aside from being interested in your topic? Do all the top books in your market approach the subject from the same perspective? If so, how could you approach it differently?

It can take courage to really stand out and be different, but it's the only way to get a book to the top and have any hope of getting it to stay there.

You can get a copy of the template I use, with examples and an explanation of how to use it at 47MindHacks.com/Gap.

Exercise: Dare to Be Different

1. List the top ten books in your market or genre.
2. Write down what makes each of them different. Niche for a group of people? Book style? Book length? Perspective on the topic? Etc.
3. Who is your ideal reader?
4. What do they have in common?
5. How can you be different? What is the gap?

The Authorpreneur Mind

"Standing out as a writer today requires more than a bright idea and limpid prose. Authors need to become business people as well."

Dave Morris (Author)

To be a successful writer and make money, you essentially have to run your writing career like a business. What does that mean? It means you have to know your audience inside out: you have to know what they struggle with, find out what problems they have (related to your field), and write with a focus on helping them solve that problem. So if you want to be successful, you have to learn to write for an audience, not just for yourself and your passion.

This is called 'writing to market'. It's unfortunately seen as something dirty by a lot of writers, who think it means you've sold out. However, nothing could be further from the truth, provided you do it the right way. You want people to buy your book – otherwise, what's the point? If no one buys, no one is reading it, so you're not helping anyone. Harsh, but true. So if you take the intersection of what your audience is looking to buy, and what you're passionate about writing, then you end up writing to market in a way both you and your readers are happy about. That's the essence of this section: the mindset you want to have around the business aspect of your writing, before you actually put pen to paper and write.

Mind Hack #25:

Think Big

"Failing to plan is planning to fail."
Alan Lakein (Author)

You often hear people say a book is a business card. While that isn't wrong, it's so much more than just 'a business card that doesn't get thrown away'. Your book is the entrance to your experience funnel that, if done right, leads to your business. It's the first step in a series of experiences they can have with you.

The reason it's not just a business card is that while a business card directs people to your business, it has little to no influence on their thoughts about your business. Sure, if it's poorly done, it will reflect on your business, but that's about it. It never provides people with an experience where they get to know you, and it certainly isn't part of a plan with ten or more experiences.

A large part of this experience comes down to branding. The trouble is, a lot of people don't really think about branding, at least not in the way that matters. That goes for both the book and the business. Now, I'm not talking about some graphic design elements, which is what most people think 'branding' is. What I mean when I say 'branding' is the essence of the book or business.

When people read your book, they associate any mistakes they find with your business. The opposite is also true: they equate the value they get from your book with the value they think they'll get from doing business with you. However, they also take away an impression of what they think doing business with you will be like. If your book is conversational, they'll think you will be easy to talk to. If it's academic, they'll associate you with being precise, intelligent, and absolute. If you have a lot of exercises and write out various action steps for the reader, then they'll assume that doing business with you will be step by step and action-orientated.

While that is all great, what if your actual business doesn't reflect the same thing? That is where you end up breaking your brand, which leads people to distrust you and your business on the subconscious level. That is why it's so important to design the experience your brand provides, and to make sure it's consistent between your book and your business.

With a well-designed experience funnel, the reader experiences one thing reading the book. They experience the same thing in the way you take them from your book into your business. Then they experience the same thing in your lead magnets (free offers) and your trip wires (low-priced offers), and finally, they experience the same thing again within your business.

If, however, your experience funnel is poorly designed, your reader experiences fundamentally different things at the different points in the journey and they arrive at the doors to your business, thoroughly confused about what you stand for and unsure what they're going to get next.

When you sit down to plan your book, or series of books, you need to arrange the entire experience beforehand. If you already have a business, then match everything to your business's brand. If you don't have a business yet, but you already have a book, then build your business around the overall experience your book provides. Make sure it's consistent for your reader, because people thrive on consistency on the subconscious level. Your subconscious hates change and does everything it can to make you feel uncomfortable when change is happening. So if your experience funnel shows consistency on the subconscious level, your readers are much more likely to follow it through, enter your business, and become a paying customer.

You'll want to plan out each step in your funnel very carefully, and all before you put pen to paper or fingers to keyboard, for the writing part of your book. Once you have your outline done, you'll have an extremely good idea about what goes into each section of your book. Therefore, you'll have a good idea of what your reader might be thinking and feeling at each point. What extra information might they need from you to get to the next step? What story or exercise will mentally move them on to the next phase of your experience funnel? Where do you ultimately want to take them?

There are numerous possibilities for where you take your ideal customer: from courses, to coaching, to engaging your readers even more with the world you're creating.

The bottom line is, remember to plan that big picture and the reader experience before you start writing.

Mind Hack #26:

Take Me to Your Leader

"A man who wants to lead the orchestra must turn his back on the crowd."

Max Lucado (Author)

One of the best things you can do for your writing business is to build a list of people who buy your books. The one thing to bear in mind, though, is that you need to control the platform where your list is held. That means that solely building a social media following doesn't cut it. There are too many ways for people to get their social media accounts shut down for you to rely on it for your business. You really just want to use your social media following as an added extra, or you're at risk of losing your business at the drop of a hat.

Building your list has to start with your own website, where you collect your reader's email addresses and build your platform. However, it doesn't stop there. A list is only useful if it's engaged, which means it's up to you to keep them interested, and continue reminding them of who you are and why they like the information you send them. To do that effectively, you have to lead. You have to be in the spotlight and have conversations with them.

Get to know your readers. Ask them what they want. For nonfiction, find out what they're struggling with and what they don't understand about your topic. For fiction, find out what they want to experience more of in terms of your world or characters. Then listen. Engagement is a two-way street. You can't lead by shouting about things. You can't lead by pushing people in the direction you want them to go. You have to inspire them, then let them decide to follow or not. Show people the destination and start walking. If your destination is where they want to go, they'll follow. If it isn't, they won't.

Ironically, if the destination is something you believe in so strongly that you just want to tell the world and then go there, whether people follow or not, you'll end up inspiring them to follow you. They can sense your passion and want it to rub off onto them, because you're fully alive and busy living it. They want to hear about what you're doing and learning on your journey, and they want to live vicariously through you.

So what makes someone a leader? Simple, they have people following them. In any group of people, like the tribe you're setting out to create, there will always be a leader. It's just the way people operate. The only question is, is that leader you? Because if you're not leading, you're following, and someone else is leading. And that leader might not be heading in the direction you want to go.

Mind Hack #27:

Permission Granted

"The future of publishing is about having connections to readers and the knowledge of what those readers want."

Seth Godin (Author)

A lot of creative people hate the idea of marketing. I've repeatedly come across the belief that, "Marketing is a necessary evil." It sometimes seems that if an author could avoid having to market, life would be a lot more pleasant.

What if one of your friends was a real food buff with a weekly podcast? They love eating out, especially in exotic restaurants, and they've just moved to your home town and need to find a good restaurant fast, before tomorrow's podcast episode. Would you tell them about that amazing, authentic Thai restaurant that's hidden away in some tiny strip mall in the middle of nowhere, even if they didn't directly ask you? Definitely. It's exactly what they're looking for. Would you feel sleazy for recommending it? Of course not, you know they'd be happy you mentioned it, and you know they needed the information. Do you think of that as marketing? Because that's what it is: word-of-mouth marketing for the restaurant.

The same applies when it comes to marketing your business or your books. People are looking for a solution to a problem they have, whether that's a nonfiction type of problem that your book or business can help them solve, or an 'I need something good to read' type of problem that a fiction author can solve. However, if the person looking for the solution doesn't know that you, your business, or your books exist, they are left with an unsolved problem.

Provided what you offer is good and worth buying, because it will help your reader solve their problem, then marketing is the path to helping people. So if you want to impact more people and help them solve the problem you talk about, you have to get your message out there, because only then can you change someone's life.

Putting an offer in your book for further information, in exchange for joining your email list, allows your readers to decide for themselves whether they need more information. They already trust you, because they've just read your book and liked what they read. So signing up to your list is their way of saying they value your information and would like more of it, please.

Why wouldn't you put that type of offer in your book? Maybe you don't think you have any further way to help them. Maybe you're a 'one piece of information' type of nonfiction author. Maybe you're a 'one story only' type of fiction author. If so, and you have nothing more to add on the topic or no more stories to tell about your world, then that offer will get you nowhere. After all, you're obviously not going to write another book they might like, because that would mean you have further information or more stories.

If, however, you do have more information or stories, and you don't put that type of offer in your book, you're essentially saying to your reader that you don't care if they want more. You're not willing to provide it.

Marketing, especially to your list, is about sharing further helpful information with a bunch of people who've already asked you to let them know more. You don't 'have' to market, you're 'allowed' to market. Coming from that perspective will make your marketing a lot more effective. It will help your readers improve their lives. Plus, you'll stop feeling sleazy and start feeling like you're helping people solve their problem.

Mind Hack #28:

Your Army on the Ground

*"Asking anyone what she or he
is reading is a necessary part of
conversation, exchanging news. So I take
recommendations from friends – and I
always pass along a book I've loved."*

Marianne Wiggins (Author)

Your readers are your private army when it comes time to get the word out about your books. They've read and love your book. They're almost certainly open to telling others about it. All you have to do is ask. The trouble, however, comes when up pops the limiting belief: "Why would they want to spend time spreading the word about my book?"

I first realized the power of this army while I was on my first book launch team for one of my favorite authors. Since then, I've been on a number of launch teams and street teams, and I've seen just how powerful a group of fans can be for getting the word out about an author or a new book.

You can spend two hours a day on marketing. Posting various promotional items to social media. Doing interviews. Writing guest posts and so on. At the end of the week you'd have done ten hours of hard work. Alternatively, having a street team allows you to spend fifteen minutes creating a post your team can run with. And five minutes asking them to post it on various social media platforms or, if relevant, their blogs. With one thousand fans, each spending five minutes, you suddenly generate eighty-three hours' worth of marketing, all done in a very short time. Plus, they are all much more likely to generate a response because they're telling their own friends and tribes about you, instead of you telling anyone.

So why would they want to do this? Have you ever read a book you loved? Did you tell anyone about it? What if you had friends who were looking for a new author in that genre, or a friend who had a problem that book solved? Would you tell them then?

I love telling people about great books I've read. If it's a book that family members or close friends would get a lot from, I've been known to buy another copy and send it to them. I still tell people about books I read ten or more years ago that changed my life. And I regularly spread the word about new books and authors I've discovered. You can probably already tell that from the number of books I've mentioned in here. I'm not alone in that behavior. In fact, I'm not even one of only a handful of people who do this. There is a large percentage of the population that loves to share books and other things they've discovered.

If you give your fans the opportunity, a portion of them will love telling their friends about you and your book. So give them the opportunity. They'd love to help, and the rewards of getting them involved will astound you.

I interviewed two PAs who run highly successful street teams. You can download the interview at 47MindHacks.com/Army.

Mind Hack #29:

Your Time Is Valuable

"Until you value yourself, you won't value your time. Until you value your time, you will not do anything with it."

M. Scott Peck (Author, Psychiatrist)

A lot of writers who are new to business think they can save some money by doing things themselves. Unfortunately, it's usually with things they have no expertise around, so it ends up hurting their business in the long run.

Most people think that if they've got time to spare, they can do whatever it is themselves. However, everything has a cost to it. If your time was free, then you'd be worthless. Since you're not worthless, your time isn't free. It's valuable. If you weren't doing that task, what else could you be doing? Well, you could be writing, which is what you're good at and presumably what you enjoy doing. Instead, you're spending your time creating your logo, book cover, or website.

A friend of mine gave me some tough love on this topic a year ago. He said, "You don't go to your next-door neighbor with your health problems just because they're free; you go to a qualified practitioner. So why do you think you can design your own book cover when you've not studied it or spent 10,000 hours practicing it?" It's a good question. One I think a lot of authors never think about.

If you want to succeed at your writing business, then you have to treat it like a real business. You need to focus on the things in your job description, like writing, marketing, and promoting, and leave the rest to someone else.

Sure, I know that when you're starting out, there is no one else. However, there's no reason why you can't be creative about making a little extra money to pay for some help. After all, you're a creative person. Ask around in your network or your local town for businesses who need some freelance writing done. At the end of the day, the more you write, the better you become, so you'll actually improve your core skill with your extra time, instead of ruining your business with it. Use the extra money you made to hire a book cover designer so you end up with a great book cover that generates more sales.

Writing

*"Writing's still the most difficult job
I've ever had – but it's worth it."*

'John Grisham (Author)'

Writing a book can be one of the biggest goals you take on. If done right, it can also be one of the most rewarding. For a nonfiction book, it can even be one of the best business decisions you ever make. It does, however, as with anything worth doing, come with its own specific challenges: from finding the time and discipline to write, to getting over the procrastination, to working out how to get your message or story across. Moreover, you have to deal with how your family and friends respond to you locking yourself away to write, not to mention the ultimate dread for a writer: writer's block. This section deals with the challenges and mindset issues you face as you sit down to write and build yourself a daily writing habit.

Mind Hack #30:

Focus, Focus, Focus

"Planning to write is not writing. Outlining, researching, talking to people about what you're doing, none of that is writing. Writing is writing."

E. L. Doctorow (Author)

To be productive and get the writing done, you have to focus and concentrate, which for most people is easier said than done. This is especially true if you're working on your own because it's very common to let Parkinson's Law come into play, which states that your work will take up all the time you allocate to it. Instead, to get more writing done, you want to do smaller spurts of frenzied activity, followed by a break. That is what will ultimately lead you to become a more productive writer.

As with just about anything, focus is a learned skill that improves with practice. A good method to help you with that is the Pomodoro technique. This is where you use a timer to work for twenty-five minutes straight and then take a five-minute break. Repeat that another three times; however, make the last break fifteen to thirty minutes long. You can easily find the details of this at PomodoroTechnique.com.

I grew up using something similar. As a child, my mother used to set a timer, and I had to work until it rang. Initially, it was very short, about five minutes. Then, as I grew up, she stealthily set it for longer and longer until I was focusing on homework for an hour or more at a time. So while I've never actually followed the Pomodoro method, I can vouch for the fact that a timer helps enormously when it comes to improving your focus and concentration skills.

What about multitasking, though? We've all grown up in an era where multitasking was considered the holy grail of productivity. A woman who could take care of the kids, look after her husband, and hold down a high-powered job, all without breaking a sweat, used to be considered the ultimate multitasker. Today, though, we're finally seeing multitasking for what it really is. A farce.

The Lies We Tell Ourselves About Multitasking

Multitasking has repeatedly been shown to slow down performance and be an ineffective use of your time. However, what hasn't been highlighted much is that there are also studies that show how multitasking damages your brain.[2] A study from Stanford University proves that people who try and multitask on a regular basis become less capable of blocking out irrelevant information. A multitasker's performance, memory, and the length of time it takes them to switch between tasks are actually worse than those who don't try to multitask on a regular basis.

The damage to the brain is even more pronounced when you're learning. A study done by Russell Poldrack at UCLA shows that anything you're trying to learn while multitasking is stored in the wrong area of the brain, which makes it harder for you to recall the information at a later date.[3]

If you're still not convinced that multitasking is a bad idea, then here's a little experiment you can try. You'll need a pen, paper, and a stopwatch.

1. Time yourself while you write out, as fast as you can, the numbers one to ten, then on the line below write out the letters of the alphabet from A to J. You are aiming to have the following on your paper:

    1 2 3 4 5 6 7 8 9 10
    A B C D E F G H I J

2. Note down the time it took. Now, time yourself again while you write a number on the top line, then a letter on the line

below, then back to the next number, and so on. Your aim is to have exactly the same thing written down, but this time you are going to swap between the two lines after every letter or number. So you'll be writing, 1, A, 2, B, and so on. Once again, write down the time it took you to do it.

Now compare the two times. If you're like me, it took you nearly double the amount of time to 'multitask' as it did to focus on each single task, one after the other.

Focus in Action

What does that all mean for you, the writer? You want to focus on a single task at a time, as that will increase your productivity. One of the ways to ensure you can do this is to cut down on the distractions around you when you sit down to write.

If you're at your computer, shut down social media, turn off your cell phone, put Skype into 'do not disturb' mode, close your email program, and turn off any other items that notify you of things as they happen. All you want to have is your writing program, Word, Scrivener, or whatever you use, and your outline open. If you use an online timer, then have that open as well, but that's it.

Let anyone you share a space with know that you don't want to be disturbed. If you write from home and have kids or family around, you need to find a way to stop them from disturbing you. If you have a door, you can simply close it and hang a 'writing' sign on it. However, if you don't, then one of the ways I've been told that works is to have a 'writing' hat. For instance, a baseball cap or even a tiara.

Make sure your family knows that when you have your 'writing hat' on, they aren't allowed to disturb you. Obviously, if there's an emergency, then you're available, but otherwise it's as if you're out of the house. Then when you're done with your focus period, simply take off your hat.

You also want to pick a specific time of day that works for you and stick to that so it becomes a routine for both you and your family. Then when it comes to your focus time, sit down and write.

Mind Hack #31:

Gamify Your Progress

*"It's play that helps us do
serious things better."*
Jake Orlowitz (Head of the Wikipedia Library)

One of the biggest mindset issues I've seen is for people to find the time to write, instead of doing other things. So if you have a belief like, "My writing is not as important as everything else my family has going on," then this chapter is for you.

This isn't really a time issue; instead, it's more of a teamwork issue. There's no way that your writing will naturally win out over a life, work, or family commitment, so the way to approach it is to get buy-in from your family and whoever is impacted by your writing time.

Anything like a writing schedule will ultimately affect the people in your life. We all only have 24 hours a day. If you're spending, say, two hours a day writing, that's two hours you're not doing something else. Unless your family or friends understand why, they're naturally enough going to push back on it, and you're going to waste your writing time feeling guilty about it. Neither of which is going to help you write.

So how does 'you being an author' help them? Schedule a time to sit down and share your vision with them for why you want to be an author. Put it in a way that shows them how they will benefit from it. If it's a creative outlet, will you be less stressed? If it's a business opportunity, will you earn more money? Whatever the reason is for you, show them how their lives will be better because of it and ask them to help you to achieve it.

You want to get them involved in the outcome in a way that even the smallest child feels like they're contributing. One way to do that is to turn your writing into a game so everyone is excited to be a part of it. Create a display that everyone can see, with your milestones and progress on. Then every time you reach a milestone, the whole family gets a reward, like going for ice cream. You can make your milestones small, like a single chapter, or you can make them bigger, like a section of your book. You can have bigger rewards for bigger milestones, like finishing your first draft, and so on. Whatever works for you and your family. That way no one, including you, resents the time you spend away from your family, writing.

You can get a template for this at 47MindHacks.com/Game. It is a Google spreadsheet, with a "Read Me" tab that explains how the automatic features work to help you stay on track.

Exercise: Gamify Your Progress

Explain your vision to your family, in terms of how it benefits them.

Set up a milestone / aim for date / progress / reward chart for the whole family around your writing so everyone can get in on the game.

Mind Hack #32:

Be a Time Lord

"Time is what we want most,
but what we use worst."

William Penn (Entrepreneur, Founder
of the Province of Pennsylvania)

One problem a lot of writers experience is finding the time to write. I've heard people say, "I never have time to write." If you look a little closer at that belief and what is behind it, you find that it isn't a time issue. It's a priority issue.

Most of the time, when you want to ensure something gets done, the best person you can give it to is the busiest person, because they understand time management. When it comes to your writing, the things you measure and schedule are the things that get done.

To make sure something gets done, you have to work out your priorities, and decide what is important to you and what isn't. The single best way I've found to work that out came from Warren Buffet. As one of the richest men on the planet, I figure he knows a thing or two about managing time and achieving things. He has a process that is very highly focused and enlightening in its bluntness, and I've recently been putting it into place in my life.

The idea behind it is that there are only so many items you can focus on and complete at one time. Anything that gets in the way of those things will stop you achieving what you most want to do. So, therefore, you need to stop doing them.

Take a piece of paper and write out everything you're currently focused on in your life. Include things from every part of your life. For instance, finishing your book, going to the gym every day, learning Spanish, and so on. Next, take your list and number them in order, with #1 being the most important to you.

Once you've done that, write your top five items on a 'To Do List'. Put the rest of them on your 'NOT To Do List'. To achieve your top items, you have to focus on them completely, make progress towards them, and let them be your guide for every decision you make. For every decision, ask yourself which answer will move you closer to achieving one of your top five items.

Your sixth item, or the top one on your 'NOT To Do List', is the biggest threat to you achieving your top five items. It's clearly something you want pretty badly, but not quite as badly as your top five.

Now that you have your priorities laid out, is finishing your book in your top five? If not, you probably now realize why it's been hard finding the time to write. You've got to ask yourself some tough questions about what you want to do.

If writing a book is in your top five, how do you go about finding the time to write? Well, it's not about finding time, it's about *making* time. The time for working on your top five comes as a result of all those things on your 'NOT To Do List'. All the time you spent each day doing those things adds up. Same with all the little extra things, like watching TV.

What you want to do is pick the same time each day and schedule one hour of 'me time' into your calendar. That is the time, barring an emergency, you get to devote completely to your top five items. If you want, you can schedule more than one block of time a day, or two smaller blocks; whatever works for you. During your 'me time', you need to focus solely on your top five items so you make the most progress you can towards the things you really want.

As soon as your calendar notification goes off, you need to start writing or working on the other items in your top five. When anything outside of your top five comes up and competes with your 'me time', you know you can automatically say no to it. So if your friends are all going to a party during that time, unless building your relationship with them is one of your top five items, writing takes priority.

Obviously, once you've achieved all your top five items, you can then replace them with your next five so your other items aren't on a 'never do' list, just a 'do not do at the moment' list.

Mind Hack #33:

Stick-to-it-ness

"Diamonds are nothing more than
chunks of coal that stuck to their jobs."
Malcolm Forbes (Entrepreneur)

A large part of becoming a successful writer is the act of writing on a regular basis. Yet, if you talk to writers about their struggles, one of the first things you'll hear is, "I struggle to write consistently." So how do you get that stick-to-it-ness that successful authors have?

Well, it comes down to creating a habit. If you remember, in the *Picking Up the Pieces* chapter, we looked briefly at the essential parts of a habit. B. J. Fogg, a professor at Stanford, outlined the method for creating a new habit. First, you need a 'trigger', something that occurs to remind you to start the habit. Then you need an 'action', which is the part of the habit where you do the work. Finally, you need a 'reward', which is what you get for completing the action.

In a study in the *European Journal of Social Psychology*[4], Phillippa Lally analyzed how long it takes people to create a new habit and turn their behavior into something that automatically occurs. Unfortunately, the results are a little longer than popular wisdom would have us believe. It ranges anywhere from eighteen days to 254 days, with the average time being sixty-six days.

While it might seem a bit disheartening, this longer time frame is actually a good thing. It means you can stop judging yourself for past unsuccessful attempts to create a daily writing habit. Maybe you did what all the habit books and gurus told you, and stuck with it faithfully for twenty-one days. Yet at the end of that time, you still didn't have anything that resembled a habit, so you slipped back into your old way of writing. This research shows you that it's supposed to take considerably longer than you were told, so you didn't fail. If you work at it this time, you'll get there.

Another thing the research found was that if people missed doing the action for a day here and there, it didn't stop the habit from being formed. That means you can let go of the need to be perfect, and stop worrying when you miss the occasional day.

So let's start building your daily writing habit. We're going to start small, because initially, without the habit, all you have is self-control or willpower. Research[5] shows that you actually only have a limited supply of willpower each day. Once it's exhausted, that's when you give in. So the more you use, the less you have left to use on something else that day.

You'll want to pick an action that won't overwhelm you. I'd suggest choosing one of the following:

- Write one page of your book.
- Write 250 words.
- Write for fifteen minutes.

The amount of pages, words, or time is up to you. I do prefer using an action that's result-based rather than time-based, though, because then you know you're getting closer to finishing your book. However, if a time-based action works better for you, go with that instead.

Next, pick a trigger for your behavior to start. That brings in what's called the 'if-then' thinking.

If [the trigger happens], then I'll do [the action].

For instance, if the alarm goes, then I'll write 250 words. That takes away the need to rely on that exhaustible amount of willpower, because you've already made the decision to follow through with the action, so you don't have to think about it when the alarm goes – you just have to start writing.

I'd recommend picking a trigger that occurs in the morning, simply to help with your motivation. That way you start your day by accomplishing your writing goal, which makes you feel successful. However, if you find you're more productive writing at a different time, then stick with that.

Another thing that research[6] has found, is that you're nearly three times more likely to follow through on these plans in the long term if you write them down. So when you've got your trigger and action worked out, write them down. Something along the lines of, "After cleaning my teeth in the morning, I'll go to my desk and write without interruption until I have 250 words." Then place it somewhere you can see it. For added incentive, tell others about it too.

Finally, you want to pick a reward that you only get for completing the writing. Following the example above, your reward could be something like, "After I have written 250 words, I get to check my email / Facebook." Or it could be, "I get to have a cup of tea / coffee." For me, I get to check off my daily writing goal on my goal tracker and note down the number of words I've written so I can see that number going up each day.

If you're the type of person who is driven by seeing progress towards a goal, that is a great reward to have. If, however, you're more the type of person who is driven by moving away from something you don't want, then the following might work better instead. Set up a chain with the number of consecutive days you've written for. Make a chart you can put another check mark on to show you've written at least one page today, like the image below. Make it so you can quickly see how many days are in your chain. You'll then be motivated to avoid breaking that chain.

1 X	2 X	3 X	4 X	5 X	6 X	7 X
8 X	9 X	10 X	11 X	12 X	13 X	14 X
15 X	16 X	17 X	18 X	19	20	21
22	23	24	25	26	27	28
29	30	31				

This is the start of your habit. Keeping it small allows you to push through and create that daily writing habit. It might take you as little as eighteen days, or as long as 254 days. Either way, you'll have a habit at the end of it and a whole stream of upcoming books that you continually write.

Exercise: Stick-to-it-ness

Pick your trigger (alarm clock), your small daily writing action (one page), and your reward (checking the task off your to-do list / adding a day to your writing chain / whatever else motivates you).

Mind Hack #34:

Crossing the Finish Line

"Book dedication: To myself, without whose inspired and tireless efforts this book would not have been possible."

Al Jaffee (Cartoonist)

"I struggle to keep my deadlines," is a belief I heard while researching for this book. A lot of that problem will be solved by creating a daily writing habit, like we covered in the previous chapter, *Stick-to-it-ness*. However, deadlines actually have a little more to them, which is why this chapter exists.

If you have a hard deadline, either from someone else, like your editor or publisher, or one you've set yourself, like your launch date, then you might have to step up a notch from your daily writing habit to make sure you hit it.

It just comes down to a little bit of planning ahead. Let's say you have 10,000 words left to write and two weeks to write it in. Doing your daily writing habit of 250 words a day doesn't guarantee you'll get there on time. Sure, the 250-word goal is a small step to get you writing, and you'll find that most days you end up writing more than that. When it comes to deadlines, though, 'maybe' is not enough.

So when you've got a deadline, you need to work out the minimum amount of words per day you have to get done to meet it. With fourteen days for 10,000 words, that means you have to write a minimum of 715 words a day (10,000 / 14).

Until you've met your deadline, keep going with your daily writing habit. However, you'll need to change the minimum amount of words from 250 to 715. If you happen to write more than that on a day, you can simply recalculate your minimum amount of words per day for the remainder of the time. Equally, if you miss a day or only manage your 250, you can recalculate again.

Mind Hack #35:

Clear the Clutter

"In the scope of a happy life, a messy desk or an overstuffed coat closet is a trivial thing, yet I find that getting rid of clutter gives a disproportionate boost to happiness."

Gretchen Rubin (Author)

One of the biggest issues, when you sit down to write, is having clutter. It could be physical clutter, like not having space on your desk, or mental clutter, where you're trying to remember to feed the dog, reschedule the dentist, and so on. You need a way to stop clutter from affecting your writing. You also need a way to get rid of distractions so you don't get interrupted, because an interruption will completely take you out of your flow and significantly slow down your entire writing session.

Researchers at Princeton did a study[7] on how clutter affects our ability to focus. Not surprisingly, they found that clutter distracts you, reduces your performance level on various tasks, and limits your brain's ability to process information.

If you find yourself getting distracted while you're writing, here are three steps you can take to reduce those distractions. First, clear the physical clutter from wherever you work. If you always write from the same location, like your desk, then keep it as clutter free as possible. It's amazing just how much those little extras tax your mind and distract you from writing. If you can see a pile of mail that needs to be dealt with out of the corner of your eye, it will mentally pull you out of your flow. So if you can manage it, write on a completely clear desk.

Second, you'll want to make sure you don't get disturbed. We've already looked at stopping people and electronic notifications from disturbing you in the chapter *Focus, Focus, Focus*. So if you need to recap, or you missed it, you can go back and read that.

Lastly, you need to clear the mental clutter. When you sit down to write, always have an extra piece of paper on your desk for the little things that pop into your head while you're getting yourself into the zone. Those things you want to remember. Simply write them on the list, flip the piece of paper over so you can't see the list, and move on. That way none of your brain power has to go into anything other than writing.

If all else fails, how about writing somewhere other than your usual spot? A lot of writers go to their closest coffee shop, simply because there are fewer distractions, so they focus on the task at hand. I personally like to go to the beach because I find that the breeze and the spaciousness of the whole area liberates me, so I get into the zone very quickly. Whatever that space is for you, keep it clutter- and distraction-free.

Mind Hack #36:

Writer's Block

*"The best time to plan a book is
while you're doing the dishes."*
Agatha Christie (Author)

This is probably the single biggest thing people think of when they think about mindset for authors. A lot of what we've gone through up to now will help you avoid ever encountering writer's block, so if this is the first section you look at, make sure to check out the other chapters if this one doesn't solve it for you.

There are really only two methods for writing a book: the 'Planner' and the 'Pantser'. Planners are super organized, write out a detailed outline, and do all the relevant research before they start writing. That way they can just bring up their notes for a chapter and start writing. The Pantser is the total opposite. They like to fly by the seat of their pants (hence the name), and write what comes to them and what they get inspired to write. They're radically different, but one of them means you should never experience writer's block.

If you're a Planner, like I am, you never have to worry about writer's block and what to do with that blank piece of paper staring you in the face. Because you never have a blank piece of paper to begin with. When you go to write the next section, you pull up a piece of paper which already has your notes or bullet points for what you'll cover in that chapter. For instance, I had six lines already written to tell me what I needed to write for this particular chapter.

Pantsers, on the other hand, always have a blank piece of paper in front of them when they start. And that's when writer's block can strike.

So what do you do? Well, my first recommendation is to become a Planner and start outlining. There are loads of books out there on how to do that, so I'll leave that to them. However, if you have writer's block right now, changing how you work in the long term doesn't fix the immediate problem.

One of the ways to get around it for a nonfiction book is to write down a series of questions that your ideal reader needs answers to. Take out a recording device, an app on your phone if nothing else, and pretend you're talking to your reader and giving them the answer for each question.

A second way is to have someone interview you about the topic of your book. This can be your assistant, your partner, or even a friend or relative. Use the questions you have written down and make sure you give them permission to add their own questions too. When they are ready to begin the interview, hit record and start talking.

However you recorded it, you now have an audio recording of the answers you came up with. You can then either transcribe it yourself, get software to do it for you (like Dragon Naturally Speaking), or hire someone to transcribe it. Whichever you pick, you now don't have a blank piece of paper so you'll be able to start filling in any gaps you find as you re-read what you said, or simply move on to the next section.

For a fiction book, you can do something similar. Ask your characters what they think they should do next. Then write down what they say. Holly Lisle covers this in a really useful way in her book *Create a Character Clinic*. What they come up with may not be the direction you wanted to go in, but you're over the blank page issue and you can go from there.

You can employ the interview technique for fiction too. Let someone in on the story you have so far. Trust them. Agree with them that you still retain the final decision of where your story will go. Give them some starter questions, and then let them run with it. Start with questions like, "What made this character start on their journey?", "What drives this character?", or, "How did this character's recent actions affect your other characters?" See where they go with the questions and what they come up with. Make sure you record it and then get it transcribed.

So how do you stop this from happening again and again? As I said, consider becoming a Planner to start with. However, if you know you are not a Planner and prefer the Pantser approach, then stick with that and keep your recorder close by to help you when you get stuck.

You also want to work out how you work best when you're writing:

- What time of day are you most productive? Experiment and try writing at different times to see what allows you to get into the zone best.
- Where are you most productive? Try writing in different places; don't feel like you have to stay chained to your desk.
- Find out what method of writing works best for you. Is it with a pen and paper? Or do you prefer to type? How about dictating it? Try out a few ways and see how you respond.

One thing I would recommend you do is always have pen and paper or a recorder on you, wherever you are. That way, if inspiration does strike, even if you're a Planner, you can quickly jot down the idea before you lose it.

Mind Hack #37:

Don't Go It Alone

*"I never won anything by myself.
I was always strong because of help
that gave me extra strength to win."*

Dan Gable (Olympian)

People seem to equate needing help with failure or weakness. The fear of appearing weak often drives them to struggle on alone. Unfortunately, the more someone needs help, the more reticent they usually are to ask for it.

Look at it from the opposite perspective for a minute, though. How great do you feel just after you've helped someone? Awesome, right? For me, just knowing I've helped someone takes my whole day up a notch. I certainly don't look down on the person who asked for help. In fact, I respect them even more because they had the guts to ask.

Most people like helping others. It's how we're wired. So if you need help, yet you don't want to ask for fear of looking weak, you're actually denying someone the opportunity to help you and feel great because of it.

Not only is it okay to ask for help when you get stuck, it's a sign of strength. It means you know yourself well. You know the boundaries to your knowledge, because no one is an expert in everything. Asking for help means you know your strengths and weaknesses. You know where you can leverage other people's skills and knowledge to create something bigger than the separate parts that went into it. It also means you're serious. Sure, with time and online research, anyone can work out how to do just about anything these days. However, is that the best use of your time? Do you value your time and yourself enough to ask for help? Perhaps someone else already knows the solution you're struggling to reach? Maybe a hand from them would mean you'd get there infinitely faster. That is what asking for help means. To me, that's the opposite of weak.

If you look at a book from a top author and go to the acknowledgments section, chances are you'll see a team of people that they regularly get help from and rely on. There's very rarely, if ever, someone who's done it completely on their own. They have an editor, maybe a writing coach, possibly an accountability partner, or a writers' group. Maybe they have a PA. Someone else designed their cover. Another person did the internal layout of the book. Their family and friends kept them going when they wanted to throw in the towel, and so on. The point is, there's a team behind the best authors. They asked for help.

To be a successful author, you need to find your team. A writing coach can help you by being that sounding board to bounce ideas off of. They'll help you organize your thoughts for the book while you're putting your outline together. They might ask you awkward questions that get you thinking in a direction you hadn't considered, but that you love once you hear it. Just helping you organize your ideas will almost certainly cut down on the amount of editing work that you have to do after your first draft.

An accountability partner is someone who will hold up that mirror if you start making excuses about why you didn't reach your deadline or your word count for the week. They'll help remind you why you're doing this and keep you going when things get rough. I have a great accountability partner, and we meet on Skype once a week. We've been through three books together so far, with many more on the horizon. Being a writer is much easier with an accountability partner, and you end up writing your book much faster than if you tried to go it alone.

What makes a good accountability partner? You want someone you get on with, first and foremost. This is the person who's going to be with you at some of the most vulnerable times of your life. They will probably be one of the first people to read what you're writing. So there's a lot of trust involved. They have to 'get you', because if they don't, they certainly won't 'get' your book. I chatted with four other people to see if we meshed before I found my accountability partner. It's a very personal connection.

You have to trust them, obviously, and value their opinion. You both also have to be able to step back and hold each other to your goals. So there's an element of tough love involved. You don't want someone who will cave and feel sorry for you, instead of holding you accountable, because you had a hard week with the kids, and the in-laws came over for the weekend, and work was crazy. Both of you need to be okay with them reminding you of your goals and asking for a commitment for the next week. And, if necessary, for a daily commitment to tell them what you've done each day.

So how do you go about finding an accountability partner? You either want to look at your writer friends or join a group of writers who are all committed to helping each other. You have to know how you work best and what motivates you so you can explain it to your accountability partner.

I'd like to invite you to join our private Facebook group at 47MindHacks.com/fb, exclusively for authors and readers of our book(s). It is a great place to find an accountability partner, and get help and support on your writing journey.

Everyone in it is a writer (both of fiction and nonfiction). Everyone is committed to improving their business around their books and helping others do the same. And we encourage everyone in there to have an accountability partner, so you can ask for people to have a quick chat to see if you mesh and want to be each other's accountability partners.

Just remember, don't go it alone. Find a team that you can ask for help, and give them the opportunity to help you and feel great about it.

Mind Hack #38:

Who Are You?

"You have your identity when you find out,
not what you can keep your mind ON,
but what you can't keep your mind OFF."
A. R. Ammons (National Book Award Winner)

One of the easiest ways to achieve something is to see yourself as the type of person who does whatever it is. For instance, if you want to write every day and put your daily habit in place, make sure you see yourself as someone who writes every day. That takes a lot of pressure off of your limited supply of willpower and puts it into the realm of self-image.

We always fulfill what our self-image says we are because that is what we really believe about ourselves. Your subconscious needs to be consistent, so it does everything in its power to turn those beliefs into reality. So if you can align your goals with your self-image, it can make a significant difference to the outcome.

There's an interesting study[8] on this for weight loss. Thirty women who wanted to be able to say no to temptation were split into two different groups. One group was told that when they were tempted to eat something like chocolate cake, they had to say, "I can't eat chocolate cake," while the other group was told to say, "I don't eat chocolate cake." It might seem like a tiny difference, but by saying, "I don't," you actually align your choices with your self-image. You're basically saying, "I'm the type of person who doesn't eat chocolate cake." Whereas saying, "I can't," puts it mentally into the realm of willpower.

While this isn't a magic bullet, the study above found that 80% of the women in the 'I don't' group were successful in overcoming temptation, as opposed to only 10% in the 'I can't' group. That's how powerful getting your self-image involved in your goals can be.

So if you're struggling to stick to your daily writing as you're setting up your habit, or you have the belief, "I don't think of myself as a writer," then the best thing you can do is adjust your self-image to include your goals.

Maxwell Maltz discusses the power of visualization as the best process for altering your self-image in his book *Psycho Cybernetics,* which is well worth a read. However, in the meantime, a quick way to influence your self-image is via the language you use when you're talking about yourself. Just like in the weight loss example, you want to use language that identifies you as someone who does the things you want to do.

When you meet someone new and they ask what you do, say, "I'm a writer." If someone asks what you're doing tomorrow morning, say, "I always write in the morning." You want to use language that shows it's something you do because you're that type of a person, rather than language that shows it's something you have to do.

So who are you?

Mind Hack #39:

Professional Procrastinator?

"Procrastination is opportunity's assassin."
Victor Kiam (Entrepreneur)

Procrastination is a killer of productivity and one of the biggest issues a new writer can have. However, procrastination has a lot of different causes, which can make it a hard problem to overcome. My question to you is, "Why are you procrastinating?" What is actually behind it? Because once you find what's behind it, that's when you can solve the problem.

There are three causes for procrastination:

1. You're trying to avoid something.
2. You're trying to do something that, deep down, you don't want to do.
3. You're lacking a strong enough 'why' for what you're doing.

We'll start by working out whether it's something you want to avoid. Let's look at what happens if you stop procrastinating. If you complete your book, or your first draft if that's where you're stuck, what is going to happen in your life? Write it all out.

- What will you have to move on to, for instance editing or promoting?
- What do you think people will start to think of you?
- What is your next big goal?
- What will becoming an author do to your self-image?
- What will happen if you finish this book and it's a success?
- What will happen if you finish this book and it's a failure?

- What will happen in your life?
- Will you have to give up that 'me time' where you were writing?
- Is your partner covering some of your chores to give you the time to write and will you have to start doing them again when you finish?

Think about every tiny little aspect of your life and what effect completing the book will have on it. As you write out the answers, it might become a lot clearer why you're subconsciously trying to delay the end result. That is then what you have to fix. If it's a mindset issue, have a look through the rest of this book, because I've done my best to cover every possible mindset issue, negative belief, or inner criticism I could think of, so chances are the solution will be within these pages. If it isn't, please contact me at 47MindHacks.com/Contact and let me know.

If, on the other hand, it's a case of you having to go back to doing something you didn't want to do, then you need to sit down and address the issue with your partner. If it's a case of you having to miss out on 'me time' or being creative, then you need to work out how to keep that 'me time' or creativity going in your life.

The second cause of procrastination is that you're attempting to force yourself to do something that deep down you don't enjoy or want to do. I call this 'should-ing' on yourself. Do you genuinely want to write? Or are you doing it because you feel you *should* write a book to help your business? Or you *should* be an author because others in your family are authors? If you're should-ing on yourself, you need to ask yourself some tough questions.

- Do you really need the book?
- Would you be happier doing something other than writing?
- Is there another way you can get the book finished? A ghost writer comes to mind. If you're simply doing it for long-term authority so you can say as a business owner that you are an author, then hiring a ghost writer would solve the problem.
- Is it just the act of writing you're not enjoying? If so, would dictating the book come easier to you? How about doing it via an interview structure? You can either write out the questions yourself, or hire someone to interview you and get the whole

thing transcribed. At the end of the day, if your knowledge is within the pages of a book, it really doesn't matter how it got there.

The final reason for procrastination is that you're lacking a strong enough reason for writing it. If you genuinely want to write a book, then go back to the chapter *5-6-7 Why*, and redo the exercises in there. Find that reason why you want to write. Make sure it resonates with every part of your being and stick it on the wall where you write. Look at it every time you sit down to write. Whenever you find yourself procrastinating, read your '5-6-7 Why' statement and get yourself fired up about your book again.

Mind Hack #40:

Are We There Yet? Write Faster

"I write four or five books a year.
That means I usually have one on the go.
I am fortunate in being able to write quickly."
Alexander McCall Smith
(Author, Professor of Medical Law)

One of the best things you can do to improve in any industry is to look outside the industry for inspiration. If you look at software development, you find the agile methodology. That is where you organize your work into blocks called 'sprints'. You basically clear the decks and focus solely on that one task for a set amount of time.

If we take this back to writing and apply it there, you get 'writing sprints'. Nothing is allowed to interfere, so before you start, you want to shut down everything except whatever you're using to write. Then you basically want to set a timer and write until the timer goes off. You're not allowed to edit, just write.

To begin with, if you can't think of anything to write, then start writing about how you can't think what to write. The simple action of writing works to release the block, and pretty soon you'll be writing content for your book. If you're still stuck and struggling with writer's block, then read the chapter *Writer's Block*.

The kind of concentrated effort that comes from writing sprints really focuses the mind and produces faster results so you'll find your writing gets faster and faster. It also helps your concentration. If you start with something that seems small and manageable, like five minutes, and gradually increase the time on your stopwatch each day, you'll find your concentration in every area of your life also improves.

When I was a little kid, just starting school, my mother used this technique to teach me how to focus and get my homework done. She didn't tell me she was increasing the time, just that I had to focus on my homework until the kitchen timer went off. Gradually, the time got longer and longer, and nowadays I can pretty much concentrate anywhere, no matter what's going on around me.

There are loads of apps available if you work best that way. Some even give you a word count, and track your daily or weekly word count. Some work with gamification to give you rewards when you reach your writing goals. There's no right or wrong way to track this; you simply have to experiment and find out what works best for you. At the end of the day, the results are all that matter. Did you meet your word count goal for the day or not? If not, start experimenting to see what does work for you.

You can find a list of apps at 47MindHacks.com/Apps.

Mind Hack #41:

Explaining Yourself

"If my books appear to a reader to be oversimplified, then you shouldn't read them: You're not the audience!"

Malcolm Gladwell (Author)

One thing you have to bear in mind when you're writing from the place of the expert, is that the majority of your readers will want a 'dumbed down' version of the high-level knowledge you have. Needless to say, when you've spent the last ten years and well over 10,000 hours working with a topic, you have such a wealth of information that you end up wanting to explain every little thing to your readers. That is never a good idea. Remember, it took you ten years to learn it all; your readers aren't going to end up at the same level of knowledge as you in the next five hours by reading your book. So you have to work out how to make your knowledge accessible and get the heart of it across.

Let's look at an example of a topic that I should imagine the vast majority of people reading this book will be completely unfamiliar with: physiology. Most people have experienced heart burn at some point in their lives, even if it's only once. However, most people equally think the solution is to down some over-the-counter medicine to 'calm the acid' and basically cover up the symptom. As an expert, you could show them that what's actually going on is something that can be reversed in a couple of minutes by a trip to a certain type of chiropractor. You see, all heart burn is, is the acid from your stomach being pushed back up the way it shouldn't be going, because, partly due to stress and partly due to the fact that you sit at a desk all day, your stomach has been jammed up against your diaphragm. Simply releasing it with a flick of a wrist will reset its position and stop the acid from flowing in the wrong direction.

That level of information is easily accessible by people without a degree in anatomy, physiology, and neurology, or five years of study as a chiropractor. They don't need to know the details of what went on behind the scenes to get the problem solved, because it won't change their lives, or persuade them more effectively. They are not interested in what had to simultaneously happen with the ligaments in their pelvis, or the muscles alongside the base of their spine, to cause the condition in the first place.

That is what I mean by 'dumbing it down'. It's not so much putting something into language a kid could understand, but rather leaving out the irrelevant bits that don't affect the end goal you're trying to help your readers reach. In this case – if you have heart burn, go to a specific chiropractor and solve the actual problem rather than suffering with the symptom. To do that, you have to know your end goal: why you want to convey the information, and what action you want your reader to take after reading it. That will help you figure out what level of detail to include and what to leave out.

Dealing with Criticism

"Stop letting people who do so little for you, control so much of your mind, feelings and emotions."

Will Smith (Actor)

How would you feel if you could write a book, or create a backend business from your book, that met precisely what your ideal customers wanted to buy? Pretty good, right? Well, that's what happens when you start looking at criticism the right way.

You have a choice when you face criticism. If criticism bothers you, chances are you think it means people don't like your book. When that happens, you probably extrapolate into, "They don't like me." Instead, you want to look at criticism as a great source of customer research. You see, when it comes down to it, genuine criticism (as opposed to a troll wanting their fifteen minutes) tells you, "This is how you could improve your book."

Sure, criticism is best approached with 'the feedback sandwich'. When you give other people criticism, this is what you want to adopt. Tell them:

1. What you like about their book.
2. How they could improve it.
3. Overall, a positive statement about the book.

Something like, "I really liked the way your book cut the fluff and got to the heart of the problem. To improve it, you could give some more examples. Overall, though, I got a lot from it."

As a successful author, you'll get criticized. Success and criticism go hand in hand. So this section is all about your response to it, from constructive criticism, right through to the trolls who simply want to provoke a response.

Mind Hack #42:

Love Your Haters

"Haters are my favorite. I've built an empire with the bricks they've thrown at me. Keep on hating."

CM Punk (Comic Book Writer)

Dealing with your haters is purely a matter of perspective. Let's take a step to the side and look at something unrelated, e.g. an old, worn-out hotel. One person might see it as a dump that has seen better days. Another person with a different mindset, however, might see it as historic. It's still the same hotel. The same goes for your haters.

At first, having people hate the book you've spent months, or even years, creating can be a crushing blow that might make you want to hide away and never come out. However, if you look at the majority of haters for what they really are, you realize how great it is to have them around.

You see, the only way your book will make any impact at all, is if you polarize people to either love it or hate it. That way your core 1,000 fans will love your work, which means they'll rave about it to everyone they know and create the buzz that you want.

To do that, you have to say something controversial. Something that readers either agree with, and have wished they could stand up and say, or vehemently disagree with, and will equally loudly tell everyone they know why. The end result is that everyone is talking about it and, therefore, you'll have raving fans and haters. The one never comes without the other.

As the author Corey Doctorow says, the worst possible thing for an author is obscurity. While it might not always be comfortable, creating fans and haters alike by making waves is infinitely more preferable to being invisible.

So when you find your first hater, rather than letting them get to you, and feeling small and crushed by it, celebrate it instead. If someone hates your book enough to shout about it, as long as you also have positive feedback, it means you've succeeded in creating a book worth talking about. That is a huge accomplishment.

The only way you'll have no haters is if you write a book full of generalized statements that don't offend anyone. That does nothing to push forward your industry, nothing to help people grow, change, or improve, and nothing to make people think. Do that, and you won't have any haters; however, you won't have any fans either. Your book will be so lackluster that no one will bother reading it, and it will just disappear into the abyss with the many mediocre, dead books listed at the bottom of Amazon.

So love your haters. They are a sign you've made an impact.

Mind Hack #43:

Don't Feed the Trolls

"I don't worry about the haters...
They are just angry because the truth
I speak contradicts the lie they live."
Steve Maraboli (Author)

Deep down, we all want to have an effect on others. It's what tells us we matter and our lives are worth something. It's probably at least part of why you became an author. The problem is, some people can't work out how to have a positive, uplifting effect on others. So to get that feedback and to feel good about themselves, they have to put someone else down. We call those people 'trolls'.

They find things that are having an effect on others. They're jealous of the author's success, hurting because they're in a bad place in their lives, or desperate for the result others are getting. That makes them feel bad, angry, or stupid, so they take out their frustration on the person they envy by saying how crappy their book is. Whatever the reason, the criticism has nothing to do with you and everything to do with them.

Trolls want their fifteen minutes of fame so they can feel better about themselves. They aim to get a rise out of you, usually by trying to make you feel as bad as they do, because that means they've met their mark and had an effect on someone.

The real problem happens when you respond to them, because that throws fuel on the fire. You basically gave their criticism credibility and told them what they said bothered you, so they will keep poking the sore spot harder and harder to get a rise out of you. That way they can continue to feel better and justify to themselves that they're doing the right thing by saying how bad you or your book are.

Here's the thing. What do you believe about yourself as strongly as you believe the sun will come up tomorrow? Those things are your absolutes, at least within your usual environment.

For me there's two things. Firstly, I'm short (5'2" on a good day). Nothing is going to change that. There's nothing right or wrong with it; it's just fact. Secondly, I'm smart and learn fast. It doesn't mean I don't have a lot left to learn, because like everyone, of course I do. There's nothing right or wrong about it; it just is. There's nothing anyone can say that will make me doubt either one. A criticism might be hurtful, but then I just ignore it because I know deep down that they're wrong. Nothing they say on the subject will affect my self-image around that topic.

What are your absolutes? Now imagine a troll was attacking one of your absolutes. How would you feel? Probably not that bothered, right? Would you reply to that comment saying how wrong they were, and get into an argument with them? Of course not. You'd know you're right. Them shouting about something that's wrong and being an idiot has no effect on you. So you'd just ignore them, as they're not worth your time or energy. At most, you'd laugh and think, "Whatever, dude."

That's the way you need to react to all troll criticism, irrespective of whether you feel utterly destroyed or mildly amused. We'll look into changing how you feel in the *Adjusting Your Response* chapter if the troll hit home.

Another problem with responding to a troll online is that you end up driving more traffic to the problem, which is the last thing you want to do. It gives the troll an even bigger kick, because now there are more people seeing their comment and interacting with them.

If you are in a place where you have control, like your blog, delete the comment and ban them. If you're elsewhere and you can ask a moderator to delete it, go for it. If not, allow your fans to come to your rescue and defend you. They, without consequence, can tell the troll they're out of line, shut them down, and show the rest of the world they were simply a troll.

The single best thing you can do, however, is completely ignore them. Show them they had no impact. In fact, go out, have a good time, and post about that instead. Let them see they're so insignificant that they're not even a blip on your radar. Eventually, they'll give up and go looking for an easier target.

I got caught up in a troll experience with my last book. I wasn't 100% sure it was a troll comment and stupidly thought some clarification would clear the whole thing up. You see, I'd written an interview book in the field of web development. We'd interviewed fourteen people on the topic, all of whom happened to be men. The market contains nine times more men than women in the first place, so there was always going to be a bias. Sadly, even though we had asked several women, they'd all said no to an interview.

Someone had promoted our book inside a Facebook group, and most people were raving about it. Unfortunately, one troll decided to latch on to the fact that there were no women and get their fifteen minutes by showing how biased against women we were. I pointed out that we did ask women; they just all happened to say no. After that, all hell broke loose. Lists of women were presented, and we were asked why we hadn't contacted them. The fact that I hadn't actually heard of any of them, and therefore they weren't among the most successful business people in the niche (which was the topic of the book), was neither here nor there.

That first comment was the only one I ventured. I stepped away from the conversation and let others fight the battle for me, which went on for two days. Eventually, the moderator of the group shut them down.

The plus side was that during those two days, we had over 1,250 downloads. I'm sure quite a few of them came from that one group, as people we'd never met jumped to our defense and kept the post promoting our book at the top of the group for the entire two days.

At the end of the day, lesson learned: don't feed the trolls. Either remove them and their comment, or let your fans come to your rescue so everyone can see them as the troll they are.

Mind Hack #44:

When the Trolls Get Personal

"I always cheer up immensely if an attack is particularly wounding because I think, well, if they attack one personally, it means they have not a single political argument left."

Margaret Thatcher (Politician)

Occasionally, people will focus their criticism on you instead of your work. Maybe they haven't even read your book but are getting paid to leave a bad review. That would explain why they have nothing better to say. Or perhaps they are jealous of your success because they are failing.

At the end of the day, though, a personal attack will cause a lot of people to doubt themselves, and maybe even to withdraw from promoting their work as much as they were planning to. So it's time to look at a personal attack from a different perspective, because you are not your work. If your message is worth spreading, then it's worth spreading no matter what the trolls say.

As Margaret Thatcher said in the quote at the start of this chapter, if the criticism is personal, that means they can't think of anything bad to say about your work. How's that for a glowing recommendation of your book? Pretty impressive, right? Out of, say, 50,000 words, there isn't one idea you wrote that they disagreed with enough to criticize it. That's a success in itself.

Now, let's look at their attack from the point of view of how the subconscious works. Because of how we process information, as we saw at the start of the *Inner Critic* section, everything someone says, relates to them. So if someone is criticizing your intelligence, it means 'being stupid' is on their radar and is something they're worrying about in their own life. They're basically worrying whether they're intelligent or not. So that is what they're focused on evaluating in everyone else. To prove to themselves that they really are intelligent, they will try and work out what everyone else has done wrong (in their eyes) so they can feel better about themselves and how smart they are.

If something you said in your book pushes their buttons, all it means is that they *have* buttons. There's something about themselves they're worried is true, and they don't know how to resolve it. That means their subconscious is continually pointing out anything related to their fear, in an effort to help them resolve the issue.

So when your book brings up something related, they attack you because they don't know what else to do. Attacking you personally is their method of reaching out for help, even when that reaching out isn't a conscious act. Their subconscious is trying to resolve their issue by getting them to label everything they can find around it as true or false.

By pointing out the fault to you, they're waiting to see if it bothers you enough to try and defend it. You've heard the old saying, "The lady doth protest too much." So when you try and defend yourself, it validates that you're worried it's true. Remember, from the previous chapter, if something is one of your absolutes, you know deep down it's not worth bothering to argue over, because you know they're wrong. By ignoring it, you're saying, "Whatever, dude, you clearly don't have a clue."

So when you see a personal attack, be gracious. It means they're hurting inside. If you really feel you have to respond, simply reply with why you wrote the book and who you want it to help. While this will have no effect on the troll, it will help others reading the interaction to see the whole picture. After that, stop interacting. Never feed the trolls; it just shows them you're worried they might be right.

Mind Hack #45:

When to Listen &
When to Move On

*"It takes a great deal of bravery to
stand up to our enemies, but just as
much to stand up to our friends."*

J K Rowling (Author)

There's criticism, and then there's criticism. Even if it's constructive and you appreciate it, there are still some other factors that need to weigh in before you take it to heart and change anything.

The big issue I see a lot is getting well-meant, constructive criticism from someone who isn't your market. Maybe it's someone you know, or a well-meaning professional. You didn't write the book with them in mind, so you have to take their words with a pinch of salt.

If it's something you agree with, it's worth either asking your audience, or taking action on it and seeing what people say. If, however, it's something you disagree with, this is the time to move on from that criticism. Simply say, "Thank you very much. I'll see what my audience thinks." You wrote your book for your audience. Their opinion is the only one that matters. No one else's. If they like it, you'll sell more books and help more people. If an unrelated person likes it, it has zero effect on your sales or the number of people you help. The only thing you have to consider is, "Are they part of my audience?"

The 'Was this helpful?' feature for reviews on Amazon solves a lot of this. If you find critical reviews that no one else has said they find helpful, then you can consider them one person's opinion. You might like their feedback, decide to test it, and ask your readers what they think. However, essentially, if no one else has said it was helpful, chances are it doesn't hold much weight and you don't want to go changing your book because of it. You can move on from reviews like that.

If, however, you get a critical review and ten other people say they found it helpful, then you need to listen up. This is where the gold is. This is your market telling you what they'd like you to do differently. This is what you can use to take your book to the next level with a second edition. Plus, if it's a style thing, it's something you can use on all your future books for the same audience. This is when you listen and respond by taking action.

In short, if they're your market, listen to them. If several people in your market agree with the criticism, take action and change your book. If it's just one person, unless you love the idea, you can feel free to just thank them for their opinion and leave it at that. If they're not your market, move on.

Mind Hack #46:

Adjusting Your Response

"There is no truth. There is only perception."

Gustave Flaubert (Author)

Sometimes, even with the right mindset in place, someone's criticism still manages to hit the mark and derail you. If that's the case, there's a very powerful, yet simple mind hack you can use to dial back the sting so you can get back up, and go back to writing and engaging that group of raving fans you're generating.

You'll need to sit down somewhere quiet where you can close your eyes for about three minutes, without any interruptions. To help you out, I've recorded this as an MP3, so you can listen along, instead of having to remember exactly what you do before you close your eyes. You can get it at 47MindHacks/Adjust.

Go ahead and close your eyes. Picture this criticism, either the words you saw, or their face as they told you, or even just make up an image of what the person looks like if you don't know. However your mind wants to represent it, is perfect. If you don't think you can see a picture, that's fine too. Simply pretend and imagine what you would see if you could see one. If all you get is a sense of one, or a feeling, or some sounds, this will work just as well.

Now, you want to change the picture so it becomes black and white instead of color. Next, turn the brightness down, like you're turning down a dimmer switch, so the picture becomes shades of black and dark gray.

Take the voice or voices you're hearing saying the criticism and move the pitch up until they sound like chipmunks, like they've breathed from a helium balloon. Now take all the sounds you hear and reduce the volume until they become really, really quiet.

Now take the picture in your mind and move it much, much further away. Make it so small you really can't make it out anymore, like a little dot.

Next, move it aside to whatever position you think represents the 'irrelevant details section'. Know that whatever you pick is the correct place for you. It could be the right; it could be the left. It could be the top or bottom corners, or anywhere in between. Just trust yourself, and pick what you first thought of, and simply move the picture there.

Lastly, you're going to anchor it in place. Hear it snapping into place like a Tupperware lid, or a lock being closed. Do this for each corner of the tiny image. Click, click, click, click. This means it can't move away from where you placed it, unless you consciously decide to repeat this exercise and move it again.

Go ahead and open your eyes.

The Business of Being an Author

"It is always your next move."
Napoleon Hill (Author)

You've written a book. Congratulations. Now you have to navigate the business side of being an author. That involves promoting your book to get sales, as well as working out what else you can offer the fans on your list to help them along their journey.

Not every entrepreneur becomes an author; however, every author can significantly benefit from becoming an entrepreneur. A lot of authors, especially nonfiction ones, go on to become speakers, and a common saying among speakers is, "The money is in the backend." The same is true for authors, whether they write fiction or nonfiction, and whether they ever stand up on a stage or not.

With your book you've created a way for your readers to enter your business. Now it's time to take action and offer them courses, communities, and other things that they're wanting to buy from you.

There are a few extra ways of thinking that will help you get more book sales, prevent you from wasting money, and make your life as an author less stressful and more fulfilling. That's what this final section is all about.

Mind Hack #47:

Balance Brings Rewards

"Life is like riding a bicycle. To keep your balance, you must keep moving."

Albert Einstein (Scientist)

A lot of authors think that when the book is published, that's it. They post on their Facebook and Twitter accounts saying, "Check it out." Maybe if they're ahead of the game, they buy a promotion from somewhere like BookBub. However, that's it. Unfortunately, that's just not the way things work. Especially if you want to build a business off the back of your book, or expand your current business.

I've heard people say content marketing is 20% content, 80% promotion. With your first book, it's not far off the same picture. Once you have multiple books, if they're in the same field, they can promote one another. Plus, when a reader goes to your author page and can see you have other books on related topics, they're more likely to buy your other books. However, the first one stands alone.

There are loads of sources of information for the tactics you can use to promote your book, so I'll let someone else cover that aspect. What we're going to do is look at the mindset you need to have as you go into the promotional phase of your book.

The first thing you want to do is to be aware of where you're spending your time. As with any business, you want a balance between the time you spend working 'on' your business and the time you spend working 'in' your business. For an author, working 'on' your business refers to marketing, promotion, and setting up repeatable systems you can use to release future books. When you sit down to write the next book, that's when you're working 'in' your business.

Common wisdom says that the best way to keep sales coming into your book is to write another book. It is true that sales of one book translate into sales of your other related books. So you'll want to set some time aside to start researching the next book. And obviously, if you're an author first, entrepreneur second, then writing is the core of what you do. If, however, you're an entrepreneur first, author second, then maybe a subsequent book isn't something you're interested in.

When it comes to the business side of being an author, you'll want to get into the analytical mindset that brings the greatest success. The heart of being successful at promotion is bringing in more money than you spend. It's obvious when you think about it. However, I find that most people don't track to see precisely what was an effective promotional activity for them, and what wasn't worth the money spent on it.

Everything about this mindset is driven by numbers, so you'll need to track your sales on a daily basis. That way, when you put any promotional activities into play, you'll be able to quickly and easily see whether they were worth the investment. Track your daily number of sales in a spreadsheet. You'll want to do it at the same time each day. Add another column to keep track of your sales rank so you can see how things affect that as well. Finally, add the number of opt-ins to your business that day. That way you'll know the normal trends for your book and business.

When you do a promotion, note down in your spreadsheet what type of promotion you did and how much it cost, both in terms of money and time. That way you'll be able to see how many extra books you sold over what you were expecting. Plus, you'll be able to see how many extra leads entered your business because of the promotion.

I've made the template I use for tracking my sales numbers available 47MindHacks.com/Sales.

It will take some time and experimenting; however, pretty soon you'll be able to see which promotions sell the most books for you, and which promotions get the most leads into your business. The two answers may not be the same thing. You can then go back to your purpose for your book and work out whether you want more sales or more leads, and focus more on that type of promotional activity.

That is when you can come up with your marketing calendar. Write out a twelve-month plan for what promotions you're going to do when. If you tie together different types of promotions, you might find they have a compounding effect. Your numbers will tell you if that's the case or not. At the end of the day, everything you do for promotion should be driven by those numbers. They will tell you exactly what you need to do to reach the goals you have laid out for your book and business.

Bonus Mind Hack:

Who Says It's a Competition?

"Business today is more than ever a question of cooperation."

Orison Swett Marden
(Author, Founder of Success Magazine)

If you've written a book on a popular topic or genre, there will be other authors with books in your niche. The question is, how do you view those other authors? Traditionally, we think of them as competition. However, what if that wasn't true? Wouldn't being an author suddenly become a lot more fun?

If you did your research correctly before you started writing, you'll have worked out how you stand out from the other books in your niche. You'll know what makes yours unique; what you offer that no one else does. This is a little easier for a fiction author, because what makes you unique is your actual story and your characters.

We all know that it's easier to sell to an existing customer than it is to sell to someone who's never heard of you before. If you've been sending people from your book to your business, you'll now be building up a list of your readers. You can contact those existing customers anytime to tell them about your next book, among other things.

If your 'competition', those authors you wanted to stand out from, have also built a list, then that is where it can start to get interesting. Rather than competing against each other, how about promoting each other's books to your respective lists? After all, with fiction, there's no such thing as too many good books. Readers are always looking for the next author they like. With nonfiction, just because an author is in the same niche as you, it doesn't mean their book covers the exact topic the same way you did. Chances are, readers will read more than a single book on a topic they're interested in.

So those authors, your so-called 'competition', suddenly become your best source of book sales. It's time to embrace them, contact them, and see if they've built a business and a list from their books. If so, you can start talking about promoting each other on a regular basis. If you're on Amazon and have signed up as an affiliate, you even get to make some extra money from a book your 'competition' wrote.

Conclusion

*"As a writer, the best mindset
is to be unafraid."*
Malcolm Gladwell (Author)

As writers we all experience that roller coaster of ups and downs. Hopefully, this book has helped you minimize the down times and get back to the up times much faster.

We looked at the mindset you need for success and defining your 'why' statement for your book. Plus, we took it a step further and covered how to find your 'why' at a deeper subconscious level so you can see what's truly driving you and use it to your advantage to stay motivated.

We covered that annoying inner critic, and its beliefs and attitudes that trip writers up, as well as a way to hack your mind to gain instant confidence and self-belief. As we saw, standing out from other authors and books in your field comes with a psychological minefield which we navigated so you can work out how to position your work.

Every writer nowadays needs to be an entrepreneur, so we looked at the ways you want to think about business before you start writing and how they affect your writing.

The next obvious step was the writing itself, which comes with a whole host of limiting beliefs, time traps, and rabbit holes to keep you from actually writing. We looked at how to neutralize them so you can just sit down, write, and produce that book.

Once you've got your work out into the world, you need to be able to deal with the criticism that will come your way, from well-meaning people as well as trolls. We looked at ways to help you see criticism for what it really is, and revealed a mind hack to help you put the painful stuff into perspective and stop it affecting you.

Lastly, we looked at the mindset you want to have around business so you can create a profitable business linked to your books and get paid for your expertise.

If you haven't started writing yet, now is the time to work out if writing a book is in your top five goals, as we saw in the *Be a Time Lord* chapter. If it is, then commit 100% and start writing every day, even if it's just a little bit. That way you will end up with that finished book.

Once you publish your book, if it's good, you'll end up with raving fans as well as critics. Enjoy your fans, but use your critics to improve your book and your writing overall. They are one of your most useful sources of feedback.

Every writer needs to build a business from their books. Whether you're a fiction or nonfiction writer, send people from your book to your business. That is how you can build your list (or platform) of buyers rather than just blog readers. These are the fans who are going to make releasing your next book easier than your last one.

Finally, join forces with your competition. If they have a list of people who read books on your topic, they will be one of your best sources of leads. So promote each other. There's always room for another good book, and readers will be more likely to buy it if it's promoted by an author they like.

For those of you who prefer to read this book, and then come back to the exercises, all the exercises are repeated in the following section for ease of use.

If you enjoyed this book and it helped change your mindset, we'd really love it if you left a review. As an author, you know just how important reviews are to getting your book known. So we'd greatly appreciate it if you spent a couple of minutes writing one. Thank you!

To connect with us more, come and hang out on our Facebook group at 47MindHacks.com/fb. It's a place where you can find your accountability partner, share your goals, get feedback on your book titles, and receive info from us on what's working right now in the self-publishing world. Only readers of our book(s) can find it. Yes, we have more books coming, and we'll be announcing them first to our list and our Facebook group. Hope to meet you there soon.

Exercises in the Book

Exercise: Read Around

Get hold of a book from an author you like. It doesn't need to have anything to do with your topic, you just have to find a style of writing you like and a book you got a lot from when you read it.

Spend an hour copying out some of your favorite sections, using whatever method you use to write your own material. So if you write by hand, copy these out by hand.

How does the author talk to the reader? How long are the sentences? If it's nonfiction, do they include exercises? If so, how much work is involved in the exercises? You want to dissect their writing as much as you can, because that is what's going to help you become a better writer.

Exercise: 5-6-7 Why

Take a piece of paper and write down a vertical list of the numbers one through seven.

Now ask yourself, "What's important to me about having a book?" / "What's important to me about being an author?" / "What's important to me about being a writer?" (Use whichever question resonates with you best.)

Write your answer next to number one.

Next, you're going to take the answer you just wrote out and ask yourself, "What's important to me about (your answer)?" And you want to write out that answer in the second slot.

Keep going all the way down to the seventh line.

To help you see this more clearly, here's an example:

"What's important to me about having a book?"

1. It will help me prove my credibility in my field.

    "What's important to me about proving my credibility in my field?"

2. It will help build my business.

    "What's important to me about building my business?"

3. I'll be able to help more people and earn money.

    "What's important to me about helping more people and earning money?"

4. I'll be less stressed and able to help people even more.

    "What's important to me about being less stressed and being able to help people even more?"

5. I'll be able to fulfill my purpose.

    "What's important to me about fulfilling my purpose?"

6. Others will get to fulfill their purpose.

    "What's important to me about others fulfilling their purpose?"

7. The world will become a better place.

As you can see, the further you go down into your subconscious reasons for doing things, the less it becomes about you, your ego, and your need for survival, and the more it becomes about others and the bigger picture.

The last three answers are your '5-6-7 Why', the reason you truly want to create your book. So write down, "I want to write a book because," and put in your '5-6-7 Why'. Then stick that up on your wall so you can see it whenever you write.

Exercise: Firing the Inner Fraud

Create a document you can easily find from anywhere. I personally use Google Docs. Write out all the things you need to do to pick yourself up when you're going through self-doubt.

Exercise: Picking Up the Pieces

Write out your trigger, action, reward, and escalation for your pick up plan.

Trigger = Something that signals you to start the behavior, like your alarm clock.

Action = Write for a short time, like five minutes or ten minutes.

Reward = Something you want, that you only get if you complete the action step.

Escalation = How you're going to increase the action a little bit each day to get back to your original habit.

Exercise: Butting Out Limiting Beliefs

Your subconscious disregards everything in the sentence before the word 'but' as false, and replaces it with everything that came after the word 'but'.

Find a limiting belief you want to change. Something like, "Nobody will want to read this," or, "My content is crap and I'm kidding myself."

Work out a tiny exception to it. Something like, "Someone will want to read it," or, "Some of it is good." It doesn't matter how small the exception is; just find one.

Combine the two sentences with a 'but' between them. For example, "Nobody will want to read this, but someone will."

Exercise: Instant Self-Belief

1. Ask yourself, "How would a confident bestselling author stand?" For one minute, stand like that. Stand up straight, with your shoulders back, and do anything else you think they would do.

2. Ask yourself, "How would a confident bestselling author breathe?" For one minute, keep the posture going and breathe like they would. Take a few deep breaths, then breathe as a bestselling author would.

3. Ask yourself, "What would a confident bestselling author sound like as they think about their books and their writing ability?" For a final three minutes, keep the posture and breathing going, and mentally tell yourself all the things you imagine they would tell themselves.

Exercise: Be the Purple Cow

Write out what each book in your market focuses on and what (from the title and cover) you think the book is about.

Brainstorm for thirty minutes about ways and perspectives in which your book could be different so it stands out from what already exists.

Knock your list down to your short list by removing the ideas you don't like or don't believe in.

Finally, pick your one item and use it to define the purpose of your book.

Pick a title and cover that express this purpose.

Exercise: Dare to Be Different

1. List the top ten books in your market or genre.
2. Write down what makes each of them different. Niche for a group of people? Book style? Book length? Perspective on the topic? Etc.
3. Who is your ideal reader?
4. What do they have in common?
5. How can you be different? What is the gap?

Exercise: Gamify Your Progress

Explain your vision to your family, in terms of how it benefits them.

Set up a milestone / aim for date / progress / reward chart for the whole family around your writing so everyone can get in on the game.

Exercise: Stick-to-it-ness

Pick your trigger (alarm clock), your small daily writing action (one page), and your reward (checking the task off your to-do list / adding a day to your writing chain / whatever else motivates you).

We Need Your Help

If you've found this book helpful in any way, would you consider going to Amazon and leaving us a review? As an author, a HUGE part of how readers find and choose our books is via reviews. It's what helps us make a living from our writing.

Go to 47MindHacks.com/Amazon, login, scroll down the page until you see a button called "Write a customer review", click that and tell people what you thought of the book (hopefully you loved it).

If you've never written a review and would like to see a quick YouTube video on how to do it, you can go to 47MindHacks.com/Review and we'll take you through everything you need to know about how to leave a review.

Thank You

I just want to say thank you for buying this book and reaching the end. So many readers never finish the books they start, so it's an achievement in itself that you're reading this and it shows just how committed you are to improving as a writer.

Hopefully you got a lot out of this book. If so, I would really appreciate it if you'd write a review, because that is what will allow other writers to find this book so it can help them too.

Lastly, if you know other writers who could use this book, please tell them about it. They'll thank you for it, and it might just change their writing career.

Next Steps

More Help?

Still feel like you need some help? You can find out more about our coaching programs at 47MindHacks.com/Coaching.

Question For Us?

If you have a question for us, we'd love to hear it! You can send us your question at 47MindHacks.com/Ask. We read every single one and we'll reply ourselves. Depending on how many people ask the same question the answer might even end up becoming a new blog post, or webinar.

Share Your Results

We'd also love to hear about your results. Nothing is more rewarding for an author than hearing how much your book has helped someone. So if you want to make our day, or just reach out and say, "Hi", you can do that at 47MindHacks.com/Share. Look forward to hearing from you!

Audio Book

For information on the audiobook go to 47MindHacks.com/Audio.

Dedication and Acknowledgments

This book is dedicated to our families and friends, who believed in us and encouraged us to keep going: Tony, Rosemary, Brian, and Maureen, thank you for your support!

David R, Andrea O, Chris W, Mason, Tom M, Steve S and everyone in our Facebook group: we so appreciate your encouragement, feedback, and opinions.

Chad, thanks for being the best accountability partner out there.

Ine, we're so grateful for your input and editing skills. You really took this book to the next level.

Thank you as well to everyone who reads this. We appreciate you more than we can express.

About The Authors

Karen Dimmick became fascinated by the brain at a very early age. As a child she secretly wanted to be a brain surgeon. However, her interests instantly changed to the less physical route during her first high school biology dissection class. Since then she's been fascinated by how people think and what drives their behavior.

She started studying beliefs and how to change them in 2004. Her interest led her to train in Neuro-Linguistics in 2006. She has been studying the mind and how it works ever since.

Karen fell in love with writing when she wrote her first book in 2013, even though she'd struggled horribly with blogging before that and dreaded writing posts. She set out determined to work out why book writing was fun, yet blogging was torture, and disappeared down the rabbit hole of beliefs around writing. This book is the culmination of everything she learned on her journey.

Steve Dimmick started helping authors in 2007. With a degree in Computer Science and a qualification as a master certified coach, Steve offers a unique perspective of technology, marketing, and personal fulfillment for the clients he works with.

He has a knack for seeing the bigger picture and uses that skill to help authors tap into a larger viewpoint for their topic. He loves coaching them through the process of creating an underlying movement that engages their readers at a deeper level.

Steve's passion is helping authors bring their works to the world so they can fulfill their life's purpose, whether they write non-fiction or fiction.

References

1. http://authorearnings.com/report/may-2016-report/

2. http://news.stanford.edu/news/2009/august24/
   multitask-research-study-082409.html

3. https://www.sciencedaily.com/releases/
   2006/07/060726083302.htm

4. http://onlinelibrary.wiley.com/doi/10.1002/ejsp.674/abstract

5. https://faculty.washington.edu/jdb/345/345%20Articles/
   Baumeister%20et%20al.%20(1998).pdf

6. http://onlinelibrary.wiley.com/doi/10.1348/
   135910702169420/epdf

7. http://www.ncbi.nlm.nih.gov/pmc/articles/PMC3072218/

8. http://www.jstor.org/stable/10.1086/663212?
   seq=1#page_scan_tab_contents

Made in the USA
Middletown, DE
08 May 2017